The Wheel of Fortune

THE WHEEL OF FORTUNE

The Autobiography of Edith Piaf

Translated by Peter Trewartha and
Andrée Masoin de Virton

Peter Owen
London and Chester Springs, PA, USA

Translated from the French
Au Bal de la Chance

PETER OWEN PUBLISHERS
73 Kenway Road, London SW5 0RE

Peter Owen books are distributed in the USA by
Dufour Editions Inc., Chester Springs, PA 19425-0007

ISBN 978 0 7206 1228 8

A catalogue record for this book is available from the British Library.

Printed in the UK by CPI Bookmarque, Croydon, CR0 4TD

Translators' Foreword

The Wheel of Fortune is the story of a climb to fame; the story of a journey from the gutters of Paris to the top night-spots and theatres of the world. This is the story of Mme Edith Piaf; a story of privation and suffering; often one of despair; always one of courage.

Wefted into the strands of Piaf's life are the names of many of the world's famous personalities: Chaplin, Guitry, Aznavour, Dwight D. Eisenhower, Dietrich, Chevalier. These were some of the people who knew her and who influenced her . . . or, as was often the case, were influenced by her.

The road to success was not an easy one. Blindness in childhood; near-starvation; life in Pigalle among pimps and whores; alcoholism; drug-addiction . . . each was a part of her life and influenced the development of her quality as a woman and as a singer.

Frequently she was hounded and exploited by the sensation-seeking Press, and she has often complained bitterly of the misunderstandings created by these 'vultures'.

Much difficulty is experienced, in sifting through all the available data, in separating truth from hearsay, for, as is true of so many who have found fame, much that is attributed to her is of doubtful origin.

On the Continent, regrettably, Piaf's intrinsic cogency has to some extent been overshadowed by scandal, real or imagined, and by the prudish superciliousness of a certain section of the public . . . that section to which Piaf herself has scathingly referred as the *'honorable societé'*.

We do know, however, that Edith Piaf's life was a pastiche of hope, misery, success, poverty, affluence and, of course, *l'amour*.

In this book, she often glosses over the more sordid aspects of her career. Even so, we believe that these things should not be forgotten or discounted, for it was the combination of the good and the bad that was the directive force in the evolution of one of the greatest *chanteuses réalistes* the world has known.

In Chapter Three, she mentions the death of her baby daughter, Marcelle. 'I had cause for grief . . .' she says; yet how profoundly must the life of the nineteen-year old Piaf have been affected by the death of this child who had been fathered by a happy-go-lucky errand boy with whom she had lived in squalor in one of the less-savoury parts of Paris. And a few paragraphs later . . . 'I had but recently emerged from an unhappy attachment'. This bald, unevocative statement almost certainly refers to her extraordinary *affaire* with Albert, a Pigalle pimp who tried, unsuccessfully, to turn her into a prostitute and who, in one of their quarrels, shot at and narrowly missed her.

Piaf's personal life was rarely above reproach and the moralists with which the world abounds missed few opportunities to point her out as a supreme example of human degradation. Be that as it may, Piaf sang with an emotional persuasion born of personal experience . . . experience without which she would have been 'just another singer'.

Intensely superstitious; a firm believer in the precognitive dream; Edith Piaf was always concious of a 'Great Guiding Force' which would see her through even the worst of her experiences.

After a period of blindness in early childhood, her sight

was restored through, she claims, a miracle wrought by Sainte Thérèse.

She had an overwhelming faith in her talisman ... her *médaille miraculeuse* ... and at one time, when it had been lost or stolen, she collapsed during a stage performance and believed herself to be at the point of death. Happily, a nation-wide Press appeal resulted in the return of the medallion and she recovered.

More than once during the last years of her life she was carried from theatre or night-club to hospital and the newspapers would announce: 'Piaf worn out!' 'Situation critical!' 'Piaf on danger list!'. Yet within days she would be back on stage and people would be talking of miracles.

Throughout her life, then, despair and disillusionment were never very far away, and it is reflected in so many of her songs. It is not difficult to see why Yves Montand once called her a *marchande de cafard* ... merchant of gloom. But if at first we are filled with a great sympathy for this little sparrow of the streets, our feelings soon changed, for she portrays herself not as some tiny thing crushed and broken by the harshness of the world, but as a wilful, temperamental, and most un-sparrow-like 'star' whose greatest love, after singing, is telling others how they should sing.

This, then, was *La Môme Piaf* ... The Little Sparrow ... about whom, in his admiration, Jean Cocteau said: 'If Piaf dies, part of me will die with her.'

Her death preceded his by just two days ....

Introduction
by Jean Cocteau

I admire the freedom with which Stendhal uses the word 'genius'. He finds genius in a woman as she steps into a carriage; in a woman's smile; in a card-player who allows his opponent to win. He rescues it from the abstract and clothes it with meaning. This means that in these women and in this card-player are to be seen all those qualities that are the epitomization of charm and grace. And so, when I say that Mme Edith Piaf has genius, I am borrowing from Stendhal. She is unique. There has never been another like her ... and there never will be! Like Yvette Guilbert or Yvonne George, like Rachel or Réjane, she burns brightly in the nocturnal solitude of the skies of France. And this star is the symbol for those romantics who still know how to love, how to suffer, and how to die.

Look at her, this little woman; look at her hands ... those tenacious, lizard-like hands. Her forehead is Napoleonic; her eyes are full of wonder ... eyes which have known blindness and now see again. What will her voice be like? How will she express herself? This tiny person ... how will she project the powerful laments of night? And then ... she sings, or, like the April nightingale, she ventures the first notes of her song of love.

Have you ever heard the nightingale? She strains. She hesitates. She grates. She chokes. Her voice rises and falls again. And then, suddenly, she sings. You are captured.

Like the nightingale, Edith Piaf explores herself and her audience; quickly, she finds her voice. In the voice is the whole of the woman; it unfolds itself like a wave of black velvet. This wave of warmth submerges us... wraps itself around us. The illusion is complete. Edith Piaf, like the invisible nightingale on her branch, becomes invisible. We are aware only of her eyes, her pale hands, that waxen forehead which reflects the light, and the voice. The voice swells and climbs and, almost unnoticeably, takes the place of the singer. From this moment, the genius of Mme Edith Piaf is seen and acknowledged by all. She surpasses herself and she surpasses her songs. She surpasses the music and the words... and us! The soul of the street filters into every room in the town. It is no longer Mme Edith Piaf who sings... it is the rain that falls... it is the wind that blows... it is the moon as she spreads her mantle of light. The 'Shadowy Mouth' — this very phrase seems to have been invented for her oracular mouth.

One

Mais un beau jour rempli d'étoiles
Mon ciel tout bleu sera sans voile . . .
Adieu les cieux couverts de pluie!
D'un coup s'éclaircira ma vie.

I can think of no better point at which to begin my memoirs than the day when Destiny took hold of me and set me on the pathway to fame.

It happened some years before the war in the rue Troyon, a very ordinary, little-known street in the neighbourhood of L'Etoile (Paris). In those days I used to sing in the streets, accompanied by a friend who, with outstretched hands, would solicit the passers-by. On the day in question . . . a cheerless afternoon in October, 1935[1] . . . we were working at the junction of the rue Troyon and the avenue Mac-Mahon. I was pale and unkempt. I had no stockings and my coat was out at the elbows and hung down to my ankles. I was singing a song by Jean Lenoir:

> *Elle est née comme un moineau,*
> *Elle a vécu comme un moineau,*
> *Elle mourra comme un moineau!*

> *(She was born like a sparrow,*
> *She has lived like a sparrow,*
> *She will die like a sparrow.)*

---

[1] Edith Piaf was then about nineteen years old. Of less than average height ragged, thin, wan, she must have seemed much younger . . . little more than a child . . . a veritable urchin of the gutters.

When I had finished my song, and my friend was making her collection, a man approached me. He had a gentleman-ly manner and bearing and I had already noticed him while I was singing. He had been listening attentively . . . and with a frown on his face. When he came to a standstill in front of me I was instantly struck by the tender blue of his eyes and his sad expression.

He came straight to the point:

'Are you crazy? You are ruining your voice.'

I didn't answer. I knew, of course, that voices could be 'ruined', but this did not really worry me; I had other troubles, more immediate, more pressing.

'You are completely mad,' he went on. 'You should have more sense.'

He was clean-shaven, well-dressed, and his manner was kind; but I was certainly not overawed by him. Like most Paris Kids, I had quick reactions and I was always ready with a prompt retort. I shrugged my shoulders.

'I have to eat.'

'But of course, *mon petit*, but there are other ways of doing it. With a voice like yours, why aren't you singing in a cabaret?'

I could have pointed out that, dressed as I was, in my ragged sweater, tatty little skirt, and shoes two sizes too big for me, I was not very presentable; but I merely replied: 'Because I have no contract.' And I added, with bantering insolence: 'If you have one to offer me . . .'

'And if I took you at your word?'

'Try me . . . then you'll find out.'

This amused him. With a slight smile he said: 'All right; let's try it. My name is Louis Leplée and I run Gerny's (a Paris night-spot of the time). Be there on Mon-day at four o'clock. You shall sing all your songs to me and then we'll see what can be done with you.'

While he was speaking, he scribbled his name and ad-

11

dress in the margin of a newspaper, then tore off the scrap of paper and handed it to me, together with a five-franc note.

'Monday; four o'clock. Don't forget,' he said again as he moved away.

I stuffed the piece of paper and the note into my pocket and started to sing again. The man had been amusing but I didn't really believe his yarn and by evening, when I returned with my friend to our box-room in a seedy hotel in the rue Orfila, I had quite decided not to keep the rendezvous.

By Monday, I had completely forgotten the affair. It was late in the afternoon and I was still in bed when I suddenly remembered the conversation with the man in rue Troyon.

'*Tiens!*' I exclaimed, 'I am supposed to be seeing that man who wants to hear me sing.'

Someone who was with me said:
'If I were you, I would go. One never knows!'

I laughed derisively.

'Perhaps. But I'm not going. I don't believe in Father Christmas any more.'

Nevertheless, an hour later I was dressed and hurrying to the Métro. Don't ask me why I changed my mind. The ex-world-champion boxer Rocky Marciano once said that when he thinks of the gangster he might have been and of all the snares that life has set for him and which he has evaded, not through any merit on his part, but simply because 'that's the way things worked out'; when he remembers all the lucky chances from which he has benefitted; he knows that Up There, there must be someone who loves him. Somehow, I can't help thinking that the same applies to me.

But to return to my story. I set out to keep the appointment, but I was quite convinced that I was wasting my time and yet, when I think back, I would not have missed it for anything.

Gerny's was located at 54, rue Pierre-Charron. When I got there it was five o'clock. Leplée was waiting for me on the doorstep. He glanced at his wrist-watch.

'An hour late,' he said. 'That's promising. What will it be like when you are a star?'

I cautiously said nothing, but followed him; entering for the first time . . . at the tail-end of an afternoon, it is true . . . one of those elegant night-clubs which, to a girl as poor as I was, was the supreme expression of luxury. Such places, where one lived on champagne and caviar . . . I could not imagine anything else being served . . . were part of a world into which people of my class never penetrated.

The place was in semi-darkness except for one corner, where the piano stood. There were two people there: a lady, the wife of a doctor, and the pianist . . . who was first-rate, which was just as well. I had no music, but this did not prevent him accompanying me with great ability. I sang everything I knew; a quite extraordinary mixture, ranging from the harsh refrains of Damia to the sugary melodies of Tino Rossi. Leplée stopped me when, having finished the songs, I was about to start on the operatic arias.

I was timid at first, but then I quickly regained my self-confidence. After all, what could I lose? After my first effort, Leplée offered a few words of encouragement and then I began to put all my heart into my singing; not so much to secure an engagement . . . this was most improbable . . . as to please this man who had taken an interest in me and with whom I now felt a mutual trust and sympathy.

Having refused to hear me sing *Faust*, Leplée now came to me and rested his hand on my shoulder in an effectionate manner which surprised me.

'That's very good, *mon petit*,' he said. 'I feel certain that you will go a long way. You shall make your debut here on Friday and I'll pay you forty francs a day. There's just one thing, though; your répertoire isn't all that it could be. You have a style and you need songs that suit your personality. I want you to learn four: *Nini Peau d' chien, Les Mômes de la Cloche, La Valse Brune* and *Je me fais petite*. Do you think you can learn these by Friday?'

'Of course.'

'One other thing. Haven't you anything else to wear?'

'I have a black skirt that is better than this one and I'm in the middle of knitting myself a pullover; but it isn't finished yet.'

'Can you finish it by Friday?'

'Oh, certainly!' I was not at all sure that I could, but my reply popped out in exactly the right tone. I had no intention of risking everything for a detail which seemed to me to be of minimal importance.

'Good,' Leplée said. 'Rehearsal here tomorrow at four o'clock.' There was just a glimmer of malice in his eyes as he added: 'Get here a bit before six . . . for the pianist's sake.'

I was just leaving when he called me back.

'By the way, what's your name?'

'Edith Gassion.'

'That's not much good for show-business.'

'I am also called Tania.'

'That wouldn't be so bad . . . if you were Russian.'

'And also Denise Jay.'

He pursed his lips. 'Is that the lot?'

'No. Also Huguette Hélia.' This was the name by which I was known in the *Musettes*.

Leplée didn't think much of that, either.

'Nothing to write home about,' he said. He looked at me

14

pensively for a few minutes, then said: 'You are truly a little sparrow of Paris. That's what you should be called, Sparrow; but unfortunately *La Môme[1] Moineau* is already being used so we must think of something else. The slang-word for sparrow is *piaf*. Why shouldn't you be *La Môme Piaf*?'

He considered this for a few seconds more. 'Right! That's settled.'

I was baptized for life.

The following day I was there on time . . . a little bit early, actually. I found Leplée there with the comédienne Yvonne Vallée who I knew had starred at the Palace and at the Casino de Paris with Maurice Chevalier. Leplée must have spoken to her of me in the way he used to speak about those of whom he was fond, because she treated me with consideration and great kindness. I was dressed like a pauper but she disregarded this and treated me, from the very first, like a professional friend . . . like an artiste. I want her to know that I have not forgotten her and that I think of her with a deep feeling of gratitude.

After my reheasal she congratulated me and said that she thought I had a great career before me. Turning to Leplée, she added: 'I want to give her her first present as an artiste. All the *réaliste* singers believe that they must wear red scarves. That is a ridiculous fashion and I am very much against it. La Môme Piaf shall *not* have a red scarf.'

She came to me and gave me her own scarf . . . a beautiful one of white silk, which I was to put to good use on the night of my début.

1 Môme: No direct English equivalent; a girl-urchin.

Friday came and I was nowhere near being ready. As far as my répertoire was concerned. I was all right. I had learned three of the songs Leplée had chosen for me although the fourth, *Je me fais toute petite,* a creation of Mistinguette, simply would not stick in my head. This was probably because I didn't like it very much; anyway, I never have been able to remember it. It was agreed that three songs would do. Unfortunately, my pullover was not yet finished; it still lacked a sleeve. I had taken it with me and on my arrival at Gerny's, I installed myself in the lavatories and knitted feverishly; at the same time running through the words of my songs. Every five minutes, Leplée would half-open the door. 'Well? Is that sleeve finished yet?'

'Nearly.'

The show had started some time earlier and at last it was impossible to delay my appearance any longer. At Gerny's, Friday was the Big Night. Leplée was eager to show off his latest discovery, but I was only an 'also featuring' in a very full bill. There could be no question of my appearing *after* the big names.

When he could wait no longer, Leplée came to look for me.

'Come on. You're next.'

'But . . . .'

'I know. Put it on. You'll have to sing like that.'

'But it has only one sleeve.'

'I can't help that. You'll have to cover up your other arm with your scarf. Don't wave your arms around, move as little as possible, and all will be well.'

Two minutes later I was ready to appear for the first time before a *real* audience.

Leplée himself introduced me.

'A few days ago,' he said, 'I was walking down the rue Troyon. On the pavement, a young girl was singing; a young girl with a pale, sad face. Her voice gripped me deep down inside. She moved me. She threw me into confusion. And now I want *you* to make the acquaintance of this child of Paris. She has no evening gown and and she only knows how to curtsey because I taught her yesterday. She will present herself to you exactly as she was when I met her in the street; without make-up; without stockings; and wearing her cheap little skirt . . . here is *La Môme Piaf!*'

This was my cue, and I went on stage. I was greeted by an icy silence which I did not understand until much later. This silence, I now know, was not one of hostility. It was simply the normal reaction of well-mannered people who were wondering if, perhaps, their host had not suddenly gone mad. And that was not all; for these people, having come to a cabaret to forget their worries, were not altogether happy at being reminded . . . at being faced with the very real fact . . . that there existed, not in some far-off land, but on their very doorstep, kids like me who truly know the meaning of the words 'hunger' and 'poverty'. Pallid, poorly-clothed, I stood out horribly in these elegant surroundings, and I was just as conscious of it as was my audience. I became suddenly paralysed with stage-fright . . . that feeling of dread, the existence of which, until that very minute, I had not even suspected. I felt like backing out but it so happens that I am not one to give up easily. Difficulties stimulate me, and somehow, just as I seem to be beaten, I always manage to find the strength to carry on. So I stayed. I leaned against a pillar, with my hands behind me and my head thrown back. And I began to sing.

C'est nous les mômes, les mômes de la cloche,
Clochards qui s'en vont, sans un rond en poche,
C'est nous les paumées, les purées d'paumées,
Qui sommes aimées un soir, n'importe où . . . .

(We are the girls . . . the vagrant girls,
We knock around, hungry, broke,
Fallen angels, tarnished pearls,
Easy meat for any bloke . . .)[1]

They listened to me. Little by little my voice grew stronger as I gained confidence, and I risked a look around the room. Faces; attentive . . . grave. Not a smile. I took comfort; I was holding them. I went on singing. Then, at the end of the last refrain, forgetting that I should not move, I made a gesture . . . just one. I threw up my arms. The inspiration wasn't bad, but the result was disastrous. My scarf, the beautiful scarf that Yvonne Vallée had given me, slid from my shoulder and fell to my feet. I blushed with shame. Now they would all know that my pullover had only one sleeve. Tears came to my eyes. My dream would end in disaster. Someone was going to start laughing and I would leave the stage amidst boos and hoots. But no one laughed. There was a long silence; how long, I don't know, but it seemed to go on for ever; and then the applause broke out. Maybe Leplée started it off. Who knows? But they all joined in, and never have *bravos* sounded so sweetly in my ears. I had feared the worst, and this success was beyond my wildest dreams. I could have cried . . . .

And then, as I was about to announce my second song, I head someone call out:
'She sings it right from the heart, that kid.'

It was Maurice Chevalier. I have received many compliments since then, but none that I remember with such pleasure.

My act over, my spirits fell. It was all too good to be true.

[1] A rather 'free' translation which lacks, perhaps, some of the innocent charm of the original.

I was only a youngster, but I had already had some pretty rough treatment from life and I was mistrustful. When you have been knocked around a bit, you come to expect nothing except more blows. That was it, then. The people out there were just mocking me; their applause was no more than a form of derision. But Leplée soon put me right. He was beaming with pleasure.

'You really had them,' he kept repeating 'And you'll have them again tomorrow and every other day.'

He was a good prophet, and at this point I would like to say just how much I owe to Louis Leplée. It was my father who gave me a taste for singing, but it was Leplée who turned me into a singer. I still had much to learn, and he was the one who was to teach me. He advised and counselled me. I seem to hear his voice yet: 'Don't make concessions to your public. You see, the great secret is to be oneself. Be *your* self.'

Being of a very independent nature, I was not one to take kindly to people who offered advice. But Leplée had such affection for me; he treated me with such consideration . . . and so touchingly . . . that I never felt the slightest resentment against him. The day came, inevitably, when I began to call him 'Papa'.

I sang at Gerny's every night. Leplée and his friends made a good job of spreading the word around and although I was unknown and my photograph had never appeared in the newpapers, people made a point of coming to hear me. Gerny's was a night-club very much in vogue and I used to see all the important people of the time: cabinet ministers (one of whom was to come to a very bad end), rich tourists, *turfistes*, bankers, well-known barristers, business tycoons, writers and, of course, actors . . . stars of stage and screen.

A proper little Paris Kid, I very quickly adapted myself to the situation and, a little tipsy, perhaps, with the heady wine of success . . . after all, it was not so long since I had been singing for my supper in the street, like Eugène Sue's Fleur-de-Marie . . I soon became accustomed to being applauded, night after night, by the most blasé of audiences.

Leplée might signal the presence of Mistinguette or Fernandel and I would say 'Yes?' and go on singing, quite unaffected by the knowledge. I thought I was good, and if I had even suspected just how much I still had to learn, I think I would have dried up completely. I would have fled rather than submit myself to the judgment of such people.

But I did not dig too deeply. I was content to savour this new happiness . . . the joy of being, as I firmly believed, a real artiste and of receiving the tributes which compensated for all the misery of my former life. There was too the pleasure of having a little money. After my first few days, Leplée gave me permission to make a nightly collection. When I had finished singing, I would go around the tables. The patrons were quite generous and one night I was actually given a thousand-franc note by the son of King Faud. It was not exactly the first time I had seen such a note, but it was certainly the first time I had had one of my own.

Of all the wonderful memories I retain of that period of my life, there is one that is particularly dear to me. It concerns the famous aviator Jean Mermoz, known to his fellow fliers as 'The Archangel'. One evening, Mermoz invited me to join him at his table. Others had done the same, of course, but always with that cavaliering off-handedness that sometimes goes with a well-filled wallet. There are plenty of people ready to 'lower' themselves, and who find it amusing to associate with a rather ordinary little singer. Mermoz was not like that, and I will never forget his first words. 'Please allow me to offer you a glass of champagne, *Mademoiselle.*' I stared at him, startled. I must have looked a bit stupid ... it was the first time anyone had addressed me as '*Mademoiselle*'. And a few moments later I had another new and great experience when Mermoz bought from the flower-girl her whole basket of flowers and offered them to me. This was the first time I had been given flowers. These courtesies, from one as great as Mermoz, astonished me, all the more because certain of the 'regulars' at Gerny's accepted my presence there rather grudgingly. One in particular, a well-known theatrical producer, advised Leplée to show me the door.

'That little Piaf is disgustingly vulgar,' he said. 'If you don't get rid of her, you're going to lose all your clients.'

'Too bad!' Leplée answered. 'I'm not going to abandon that kid ... even if it means closing Gerny's altogether.'

There was also an incident ... which I did not know about at the time ... with one of Leplée's co-directors. This man who for some obscure reason hated me, presented Leplée with an ultimatum.

'It's Piaf or me. The choice is yours.'

He left. I stayed.

Leplée, who loved me like a father, assured me repeatedly that I had talent, and yet, when I think of the way in which I sang in those days, I have to confess that my 'talent' was of an extremely dubious nature.

Many of the people who came to hear me sing were not in the least interested in the way I interpreted my songs, I discovered this one night when I was engaged to appear at a dinner-party given by Jean de Rovera, the director of *Comœdia*.

It was a very grand affair presided over by a cabinet minister, and Jean de Rovera (whose true name was Courthiadès) fancied the idea of presenting to his guests the quaint little singer from Gerny's ... this nine-day-wonder who simply had to be seen before she returned to the gutters from which she had come.

I took my accordionist with me. I was wearing a roll-neck sweater and my knitted skirt.

I started to sing to them, but they soon made me understand that they were not really interested in my songs. I was a sort of phenomenon, a curious sample of humanity, something of a freak, and I had been brought there just to be laughed at. They had been told that I was funny, and every time I opened my mouth or made some little gesture, they burst out laughing . . . .

'How drôle she is . . . absolutely priceless . . . and so natural with it . . . .'

I was the clown of the evening. They just made fun of me, although I don't think they meant to be cruel. But their thoughtlessness turned the whole thing into a dreadful ordeal. I went back to Leplée in tears and threw myself into his arms.

'If only you knew, Papa! They all mocked me. I'm no good at all. I know nothing and yet I thought I was an artiste.'

Leplée comforted me.

'If you realize that, *ma petite*, you'll be all right. You have to know your short-comings before you can do anything about them. It's all a question of will-power and hard work. I have no fears where you are concerned. You'll make it.'

Two

J'ai rêvé de l'étranger
Et, le coeur tout dérangé
Par les cigarettes,
Par l'alcool et le cafard,
Son souvenir chaque soir
M'a tourné la tête . . . .

I quickly adapted to my new way of life. I knew that it was only by an extraordinary stroke of luck that I had got this far; it was up to me to see to it that I never went back to the miserable existence from which Leplée had rescued me.

I still went around with the same old friends, but I had left Belleville and now had a room in a hotel not far from Pigalle. Although I stayed in bed late every day, I used to take my profession very seriously and I would spend each afternoon making the rounds of the music publishers. I had realized that as a singer I needed my own répertoire . . . songs which would be recognized as belonging to me. It did not take me long to find out that to build such a répertoire was no easy task.

I would not want to speak ill of the music publishers. I have among them some very good friends and I know now that they were wise to use prudence in the exercise of their business. The quickest way of going bankrupt is to be over-enthusiastic to the point where caution and common-sense no longer rule. Much capital can be involved in the launching of a new song and risks have to be taken.

However good a song might seem to be, there can be no guarantee that it will be a 'hit'.

A novelist has his faithfuls . . . several thousand readers who will buy his latest work immediately it appears. His publisher, when he sends the manuscript to the printer, is already certain of its commercial value; he knows that, come what may, he will sell so many thousand copies and not lose his money. But in the song-world, things are quite different, you take risks and hope for the best. Very often, the song that you are most doubtful about becomes popular, while the great masterpiece that you have relied on to recuperate your losses is a flop. Music publishers are well aware of this and they are duly circumspect. Knowing what I now know, I cannot blame them for not welcoming me in those early days.

I misguidedly believed that I was good enough to launch new songs. I was not making records and I had not yet broken into radio or music-hall; in short, I was almost unknown. The songs I was allowed to sing were those already used by other singers who had not retained the exclusive rights. I should have been grateful.

I understand all this now, but at the time I often felt like storming out; instead, bitter and full of self-pity, I poured out my troubles to Leplée.

'By the time they notice me, I won't need them,' I used to say. 'C'est la vie!' he would answer philosophically. 'And the funny thing about it is that when you are famous, they'll all claim that you couldn't have made it without their help.'

The following day, with new confidence, I would try again.

For a song that would really be my own, I would have done just about anything . . . as the story of *L'Etranger* will show.

One day I was at the publishing house of Maurice

Decruck, on the boulevard Poissonnière. Decruck was one of the first to have confidence in me and to be friendly. The pianist and I had been running through a few songs, none of which pleased me, when in walked a fair-haired lady, poised, elegant, who had come to rehearse a few numbers in preparation for her next performance. It was Annette Lajon.

Maurice Decruck introduced us, and, the usual pleasantries having been exchanged, I retired discreetly to a corner of the room. Her first song was *L'Etranger*.

> *Il avait un regard très doux,*
> *Des yeux rêveurs, un peu fous,*
> *Aux lueurs étranges . . . .*
>
> (*His eyes were soft,*
> *Dreamy, yet with a touch of madness*
> *And a strange glint . . . .*)

This song, quite new to me, was one of the first . . . and one of the most beautiful . . . composed by my good friend Marguerite Monnot who was, however, unknown to me at the time. It overwhelmed me. Everything around me seemed to vanish: the walls with their brightly coloured posters; the music-racks; Decruck himself, standing beside me with his hand on the back of my chair; these things were no longer there. It was like a blinding flash of light . . . like a sudden blow to the solar plexus.

This song, with its simple words, expressed the sentiments I had so often felt myself. I knew that this was a song into which I could put everything . . . When Annette Lajon had finished, I went over to her.

'Oh! Madame . . . please sing it again. It is so beautiful.'

Suspecting nothing, a little flattered perhaps, she went through it once more. I listened attentively; missing not a note or syllable . . . and I even had the audacity to ask for it a third time. She did not refuse. How could she have known that as she sang, I was learning the song?

Not wishing to arouse suspicion, I did not stay to hear the remainder of the rehearsal, but hung around in the director's office, determined to talk with Maurice Decruck as soon as he was free. When Annette Lajon had gone, I launched my offensive.

'Decruck, would you be very nice! Let me have *L'Etranger!*'

He looked at me regretfully.

'As much as I like you, *mon petit,* I can't possibly do that. Why don't you sing . . . .'

I didn't let him continue.

'No! That's the one I want; nothing else!'

'Look, it's a new song. Annette has only had it one week and naturally she wants to keep it to herself for a while.'

'But I've *got* to have it. Anyway, I *know* it!'
'You do?'

'Yes . . . all except one or two words which I can work out for myself.'

Decruck shrugged his shoulders.

'Oh, please yourself. I don't want to know. I wash my hands of the affair.'

Decruck was an honest man. I don't know what more I expected, but I was annoyed with him.

When I arrived at Gerny's that evening, I announced triumphantly to Leplée that I had a truly sensational song.

'Let's see it, then,' he said.

I had to confess, not without some embarrassment, that I had not been able to come to an agreement with the publisher and that I didn't even have the sheet-music of this song which I so unhesitatingly called 'mine'.

'But,' I said, 'I know it and I shall sing it tonight.'

He objected on the grounds that my accompanist would need the music.

'Don't worry, Papa,' I said, 'everything will be all right.'

I knew that I could count on the pianist at Gerny's; Jean Uremer, if my memory serves me well. I only had to hum through the song three or four times and he was able to improvise a very acceptable accompaniment.

And so, that evening, I sang *L'Etranger*.

I had not been mistaken in my estimate of the quality of the work. Neither had I been wrong in thinking that although it had not been written for me, it was exactly right for my personality. I had scored a hit... and *L'Etranger* was to remain part of my répertoire for a very long time.

A few days later, Annette Lajon came to hear me sing. I did not learn of her presence until I had finished singing, and then rather ill at ease, I went to her table. She was offhand and I admit that she was justified.

'You must be furious with me,' I said.

She smiled.

'Not at all! *L'Etranger* is such a beautiful song that I am certain I would have done the same thing had I been in your place.'

She was just being charitable; I know that with her kind nature she could never have done anything as bad. I was very happy for her when, not long after, her recording of the song brought her *Le Grand Prix du Disque*.

It was through Leplée that I was booked for my first gala appearance; at the Cirque Medrano, on the 17th February, 1936 ... a date that I will never forget.

The evening had been arranged for the benefit of the widow of Antonet, the great clown who had recently died. The programme-cover had been specially designed by Paul Colin and the show opened with an informal chat by Marcel Achard. All the big names from the theatre, the cinema, the circus and the world of sport were there and it was indeed a proud little singer who saw her name on the programme, sandwiched between those of Charles Pélissier and Harry Pilcer (in alphabetical order) in letters of the same size as those of her 'fellow-artistes' Maurice Chevalier, Mistinguette, Préjean, Fernandel and Marie Dubas. Leplée was escorting me and we formed a rather curious couple; he, very tall and smart in his well-cut evening dress, and me, very small, very *'Belleville-Ménil-montant'* in my pullover and my knitted skirt. I went on towards the end of the first half. I was very excited ... naturally; this was my first contact with the world of *grandes premières* . . . and absolutely determined to give of my best; to show myself worthy of the honour bestowed on me. I don't think anyone was disappointed.

Afterwards, Leplée embraced me.

'You're only a little'un,' he said, 'but you are as big as they come.'

Well-guided, working hard, I began to make progress. My name was becoming known in the profession. I had made, for Polydor, my first record, *L'Etranger,* and my photograph could be seen alongside those of Annette Lajon and Damia. I was as yet unknown to music-hall directors but I had made my radio début and after my first broadcast I had signed a ten-week contract for Radio-Cité. Jacques Bourgeat . . . my dear 'Jacquot' of whom I shall speak later . . . had presented me with the first song ever to have been written specially for me; a beautiful poem called *Chant d'habits* set to music by the composer Ackermans. I was happy and felt that I was on the way to the top.

'And it's only the beginning,' Leplée told me. 'In three weeks' time we are off to Cannes; you are booked to appear at the *Bal des Petits Lits Blancs* . . .'[1]

---

[1] A charity ball for the benefit of waifs and strays.

Three

Il a roulé sous la banquette
Avec un p'tit trou dans la tête,
  Browning, Browning....
Oh! ça n'a pas claqué bien fort,
Mais tout de même il en est mort,
  Browning, Browning....
On appuie là et qu'est-ce qui sort
Par le p'tit trou? Madame la Mort,
  Browning, Browning....

Leplée was making great plans for me, and he was pleased with the prospects of taking me to Cannes and introducing me to splendours of The Riviera. But it was not to be for tragedy was not far off. Leplée's days were numbered ... as he himself knew.

One morning he came to me and told me of a frightening dream he had had.

'I saw my poor mother,' he said, 'and she spoke to me, saying "You know, Louis, the time has come. You must prepare yourself for I shall soon come to fetch you".'

I tried to explain to him that dreams are just dreams and nothing more.

'Perhaps you are right, *Mon Petit*,' he said, 'but you must understand that it was no ordinary dream. I saw my *mother*. She is waiting for me. I have a feeling that I shall soon die. What grieves me is that you still need me. People are going to hurt you and I shall not be around to protect you."

I chided him for being so gloomy, saying that once at Cannes, this mood of depression would soon disperse.

A week passed. At about one o'clock in the morning on the sixth of April, I kissed Papa Leplée goodnight when I left Gerny's. He reminded me that I must be in good shape for my appearance, later that day, at the Music-Hall des Jeunes, a Radio-Cité broadcast from the vast Pleyel auditorium, and that I was to pick him up at his home at ten o'clock for a walk in the Bois.

'So,' he concluded, 'go to bed early.'

I lied to him, saying that I would go straight home, and then off I went to Montmartre to meet some friends. One of them was joining the army and we were celebrating his last night in town. We spent a gay night in the clubs of Pigalle and it was after eight when I decided to go home to bed. Not wanting to lose sleep by meeting Leplée at ten, I telephoned him to make my excuses.

'Allô! Papa?'

'Oui.'

'Look Papa, I'm sorry to disturb you so early, but I've had no sleep at all ... I'll explain why later ... and I really don't feel like going for a walk. If you wouldn't mind ...' A stern voice interrupted me:

'Come here immediately ... right away!'

'All right! I'm coming.'

One thought was in my mind; Papa had called me 'vous' instead of 'tu', he must be very angry with me. It certainly did not occur to me that it was not Leplée who had answered the phone. It meant losing all my sleep and I'd make a mess of my broadcast, but if Papa wanted me I had to go. I jumped into a taxi and directed the driver to take me to Leplèe's home on the avenue de la Grande-Armée.

A small crowd had gathered outside the building and was being held back from the doors by the police. Although Leplée was not the only tenant in the house, a feeling of uneasiness came upon me. I gave my name to the inspector at the door and rushed to the lift . . . a policeman close on my heels.

'Are you Piaf?' he demanded as the lift started upwards.

'Yes, I am.'

I had the idea that he was a journalist and I expected more questions; but he remained silent, staring at me as if to ensure that he would recognize me if we ever met again.

The door of Leplée's apartment was open. In the entrance-hall, strange people were talking in low voices. Laure Jarny, the 'hostess' at Gerny's was sobbing in an armchair; it was she who broke the news to me.

'It's horrible! Leplée has been murdered!'

It is impossible to describe the feeling of total emptiness, of unreality, that left me senseless, paralyzed, in a world which was crumbling around me. People were coming and going; some spoke to me, but I could not answer. Everything passed from my comprehension; I was like a corpse in the land of the living.

Looking like one crazed and walking stiffly as if in a dream, they told me later, I went into Leplée's bedroom. He was lying on his bed. The bullet had entered his eye, leaving his handsome face unmarked. I sank on to the bed and wept.

The next few days were terrible. I wanted to lock myself in my room; see no one; cry away the pain; but a police investigation leaves no room for personal sorrows.

Leplée's death was shrouded in mystery and, having no clues, Commissaire Guillaume decided to interrogate everyone even remotely connected with Gerny's or its late director: his friends, the staff, artistes, club regulars, the lot . . . including the comedian Philippe Hériat who was to become one of France's leading novelists and, incidentally, one of the most photogenic members of *L'Academie du Prix Goncourt*.

I was taken to the Police Judiciare where I was questioned for hours at a stretch by inspectors who insisted that I was not being interrogated and that the questioning was merely for my 'statement'. There was, presumably, a subtle difference; they did not, so it seemed, suspect me of actually firing the shot, but was I not involved in some sort of complicity? Towards evening, Guillaume himself took over. It took him about half an hour to conclude that I knew nothing and I was permitted to go home. However, I was 'requested', so to speak, to hold myself at the convenience of the Authorities and to keep them informed of my whereabouts.

Exhausted, I started walking and eventually, and quite unintentionally, I arrived at Gerny's. It was closed, of course, but a few people were there: waiters, the head-waiter, the flower-girl, and a few of the artistes currently appearing. One of these, whom I choose to keep anonymous, said sarcastically: 'Your protector is dead. With your talent, it won't be very long before you're back on the streets.'

Already I could see signs of ingratitude. Leplée had been a kind man. He had been sensitive to the distress of others and generous with the money he had so easily made. There were many in Paris who were greatly indebted to him . . . yet not one of these attended his funeral.

I also began to lose friends. I was involved in a scandal. Terrible things were being printed about me, and many thought it best to avoid me. The list of those who stood by me is not very long . . . and I am certain that I have omitted no one. Jacques Bourgeat, Juel the accordionist, J. N. Canetti, my ever-faithful Marguerite Monnot, Raymond Asso, whom I hardly knew, and Germaine Gilbert, the blonde singer who was with me Gerny's . . . they were the only ones.

Although I was never asked to go back to the Police

Judiciare, the investigation was by no means over and the case was to remain open for some months. During this time, the affair furnished the press with abundant copy and those people who love to glut themselves on sensationalism had their fill. Evidence was scant, but the reporters, experts in *littérature d'imagination*, were in no way deterred by this and I could not open a newspaper without trembling in fear of finding some new infamy concerning the friend I had lost or about myself. They even invented a dramatic serial-story in which I appeared as the heroine . . . a quaint but frankly unappealing character who, if one read between the lines, was the accomplice of the murderers if not the actual perpetrator of the crime. They did not spare me. I had wanted to see my name in print. My wish had been granted with a vengeance!

If I had had money, I would have fled to the other end of the world. But I had none. My meagre savings had been used up and I could see no alternative to carrying on with my career as a singer. Gerny's was closed and there was no hope that it would re-open. Even so, offers were not lacking. A number of cabaret-managers, speculating on the insatiable curiosity of the public and knowing also that I was not in a position to demand a very large fee, offered me contracts. I could take my pick.

I chose to make my come-back at O'dett's in the place Pigalle. That first night was yet another that I am unlikely ever to forget. I was greeted with a glacial silence. There was not the slightest reaction from the audience; not a single 'bravo', not even a whistle.[1] I began to sing but no one was really listening . . . I might as well have sung a few psalms; they wouldn't have noticed the difference. They hadn't come to hear a singer; they had come to see the woman in the Leplée affair. I could feel their staring eyes, and I tried to imagine what they were saying about me behind their champagne glasses:

'She was one of the chief suspects, you know. The police held her for forty-eight hours . . ."

'There's no smoke without fire!'

'Anyway, no one knows who she is or where she came from. Piaf! What sort of a name is that?'

Every night was the same and at last I began to ask myself if this, perhaps, was a new vogue. Was it now 'the done thing' to go to O'dett's for the purpose of not applauding; to teach a lesson, rather, to this little singer who dared to appear in public after being involved in a scandal?

And then one day, at the end of my first song, someone whistled.[1] Tears came to my eyes.

At one of the tables, a man, tall, distinguished, in his sixties, rose to his feet.

'Why do you whistle, Monsieur?' he asked.

The other laughed.

'Don't you read the newspapers?'

'Yes, monsieur, I do. But I do not presume that I have the right to judge my fellow men. If they are free, I assume they are innocent; if they are not free, then I leave it to the judges to decide on their punishment. The artiste you have been hearing is either a good singer or a bad one. Whistling is in bad taste in a cabaret, so if she is bad, be quiet. If she is good, applaud her, and keep your nose out of her private life which is no business of yours.'

Having spoken, my gallant defender, whom I had never seen before, sat down. People started to clap him and then, as he joined in, the applause was all for me.

Matters were beginning to turn to my advantage and I was able to face my difficulties with new-found zest. However, I had decided not to renew my contract with O'dett's and a few days later my association with that club came to an end.

[1] Here, Piaf refers to the characteristic shrill whistles of disapproval rather than those of acclamation so familiar in this country.

Then, J. N. Canetti, whose friendship had been a source of great comfort, arranged for me to tour the suburban cinemas as an 'added attraction'. I was never quite sure of my reception, but I always had a certain amount of support from those who wanted to hear me sing and who were determined to get their money's worth, and I was never booed off the stage.

The perpetual struggle was exhausting me and I began to hate Paris. I went to the provinces where Lombroso, the impresario, had obtained bookings for me. For a long time I was in Nice ... singing at the Boîte à Vitesses, a cabaret situated in the basement of Maxim's and managed by Skarjinski. I was happy there. The local papers had hardly mentioned the Leplée affair and I began to feel free once more.

Financially, however, I was doing far from well. Each night after the show I went to the Nègre in the passage Emile-Negrin for a meal, and as steak was expensive, I usually ate a plate of spaghetti.

Shortage of money is inconvenient but not disastrous. Losing the will to live is far worse, and I had almost reached that stage. With the death of Leplée, I had lost the guidance that I so sorely needed and, most of all, a sincere, affectionate and irreplaceable friend.

Our first meeting had seemed like an act of providence. Leplée, heartbroken over the death of his mother ... he had no other relations and no real friends although he seemed to know everyone in Paris ... was leading an eventful and apparently happy life; but he was alone. I too had cause for grief at this time as my two-year-old daughter Marcelle had recently died of meningitis, and our loneliness formed a bond between us. Together we had visited the graves of my child and his mother in the Cimetière de Thiais.

'They wanted us to meet,' Leplée told me, 'so that we would no longer be alone.' And indeed, we had found in each other the affection and friendship we both needed.

Now that Leplée was gone, what was there left for me? I used to ask myself this question over and over again.

Love? I was not interested. I had recently emerged from an unhappy attachment and this only added to my near-suicidal depression. My profession? Not even that! I seemed to have lost interest. All ambition was gone and I had not learned a new song or practised for weeks. Completely exhausted, physically and mentally, lacking will-power, I realized that before long I would be back on the streets as someone had predicted after the death of Leplée.

My contract in Nice expired. I returned to Paris and the very next day I telephoned Raymond Asso.

'Raymond, will you look after me?'

The tone of his voice reassured me.

'Do you have to ask that?' he said. 'I've been waiting a whole year for the chance. Just take a taxi and come.'

I was saved.

Four

J'sais pas son nom, Je n'sais rien d'lui,
Il m'a aimée toute la nuit,
  Mon légionnaire!
Et me laissant à mon destin,
Il est parti dans le matin,
  Plein de lumière!,
Il était minc', il était beau,
Il sentait bon le sable chaud,
  Mon légionnaire!
Y avait du soleil sur son front
Qui mettait dans ses cheveux blonds,
  De la lumière!

I had first met Raymond Asso when I had been singing at Gerny's. I was at the music publisher Milarski's, when a man who happened to be there sat down at the piano and played through a song he wanted me to hear. With my usual lack of diplomacy, I told him that although the words pleased me, I didn't think much of the melody ... I was not to know that he had composed the music, and he was tactful enough not to tell me so.

'In that case,' he smiled, 'you should congratulate the man who wrote the words; there he is, sitting on the settee.' That man was Raymond Asso, long, sinewy, bronzed and black-haired. He was sitting, calm, inscrutable, amused by the scene. He stood up and we chatted for a while, liking each other from the start, and I had a strange feeling that it would not be long before we met again.

I was not mistaken. Three days later, early in the afternoon, I was lounging around in my room in the Hôtel Piccadilly, in rue Pigalle, when I was called to the telephone. It was a friend, a porter in a large café.

'I have someone with me,' he said, 'who met you recently at a publishers' office. He's getting all excited and says he must speak to you. I'm putting him on . . .'

I recognized the other voice at once and anyway I'd already guessed from the introduction. It was Raymond Asso. He explained that he believed he could write the sort of songs that would meet with my approval and finished with an invitation to dinner the following day. I accepted.

Raymond Asso had come into my life.

And now I had come back to Paris disheartened, beaten. Raymond determined to restore my lost confidence. What if I had been slandered, insulted, dragged through the mud! I was not the first to hit a rough patch. One must fight! Raymond, with a sincerity and tenacity which inspired me, did most of the fighting for me.

He argued that a singer should not seek to carve a career from cabaret work. She should aim at the music-hall, for only there does she make direct contact with the real public; only there can she show her true measure and, by experience, make real progress. He was right!

I was already known in cabaret and on the radio . . . J. N. Canetti, *directeur artistique* at Radio-Cité had helped me there . . . and now I just had to strive for the A.B.C. (the pinnacle of French music-hall).

At first, Mitty Goldin, who later became a good friend, was adamant that he wanted nothing to do with me. But Asso's tactics gradually wore him down. Every morning he would go to Goldin's office in the boulevard Poissonnière;

and every morning he would be sent away. This went on until Goldin got tired of it and gave me a contract just to get rid of Raymond. I had broken into music-hall. Let no one accuse me of lacking humility when I add that Mitty Goldin never had cause to regret it.

Once again the newspapers spoke of me; this time, however, with words of praise. Writing in *L'Intransigeant*, the late Maurice Verne said:

La môme Piaf is the wistful and impetuous spirit of *musette*. Everything about her is suburban, and yet how much she reminds us of the Claudine of the 1900's! Oh, Colette! In this little singer, your Claudine, with her bob, her white cravat and her little black dress like a schoolgirl's uniform, is miraculously brought to life.

La môme Piaf has great skill: her voice can mount to a metallic, almost tinny pitch, and one imagines her, as a street-singer, singing in tenement courtyards. La môme Piaf — so far, thank God — has not turned 'literary', but she does need songs that are truly hers, with that daylight-realism which lingers in the streets of la Villette, greyed with the soot of factory chimneys, and vibrant with music from café wireless sets.

And Raymond Asso wrote songs like this for me; direct, sincere, without literary pretensions; 'as welcoming as a handshake', as Pierre Hiegel once said. The style was new, and the name *réaliste* was quickly (and quite wrongly) attached to it. Asso prefers the word 'truistic' but in fact the term itself is of little importance. It is sufficient that Raymond Asso has made his mark in the history of the French *chanson*. He inovated and influenced his followers, Henri Contet and Michel Emer for example.

In the foreword to his book *Songs Without Music*, Asso says 'I disciplined myself:

Firstly, to write nothing unless I have something to say.

Secondly, to write only of real life in the purest way possible.

Thirdly, to write as simply as I could so as to put myself within reach of everybody.

In his songs, *Paris-Méditerranée, Elle fréquentait la rue Pigalle, Je n'en connais pas la fin, Le Grand Voyage du pauvre nègre, Un jeune homme chantait,* and all the others, these three basic rules are followed, and this is one of the reasons why the songs are ... and will remain ... masterpieces. The other reason, of course, is that Asso is a great poet.

One of his best songs, *Mon Légionnaire,* was inspired by a story, a reminiscence, I had recounted to him.

It happened when I was seventeen. Some months earlier, eager to be free and independent, I had left my father with whom, during the greater part of my childhood, I had travelled around the country, putting on little shows in the streets and market-places. Now, after many unhappy experiences, I had become the manager of a small travelling troupe. There were only three of us, all about the same age; Camille Ribon, a circus acrobat who was unequalled at standing on his thumbs on the edge of a table; his 'wife' Nénette who was also his assistant; and myself. I was the singer and used the name 'Miss Edith' ... 'Miss', because it added an international flavour that is so important in variety work. We used to perform in army barracks. This had been an idea of my father's years before and I had found it worth adopting. Initially we had to get hold of the General, not always a simple matter, in order to obtain from him the authorisation to present to his men our 'recreative diversion'. Permission was rarely refused and it only remained to arrange a suitable date, time and locale with the Colonel. Nine times out of ten he would say 'Tomorrow in the mess-hall after soup.'

On the day in question we were appearing in the barracks at the Porte des Lilas where the colonial troops were stationed. I was cashier; that is to say I stood at the mess-hall door with a tin, collecting the twenty *sous* entrance-fee from each soldier. The tin was filling up nicely, when along came a handsome, fair-haired man who calmly announced that he had no money but that, if I had no objections, he was willing to pay with a kiss. I pretended to be offended and just stared at him. He was not very tall but looked strong. Untidy, with his cap perched jauntily on one side of his head and a cigarette stuck to his lip, he had beautiful features and his eyes were a magnificent pale blue.

'Well?' he said.

I told him to go through.

'As for the kiss,' I added, 'we'll talk about that later, if you behave yourself in the meantime.'

And that evening I sang for him alone!

After the show he pretended not to notice me; so off I went. He caught up with me in the yard outside and kissed me in the moonlight. Then he took my hand and began to talk ... and talk ... and talk ... he was still at it when 'lights out' sounded. As we parted he said:

'My name is Albert C ..., Number Two Company. Come here tomorrow evening at seven.'

I walked home, singing all the way. In the richness of a new-found love, I forgot my poverty. I felt that I was on the threshold of great happiness and I began making plans for the future.

The next evening at seven I was at the barracks; but Albert, so I was told at the guardroom, was in the cells.

'But what has he done?'

41

'He was fighting last night in the barrack-room. There's no need to worry about him. He knows what it's like in jug . . . he's hardly ever out of it. Blasted trouble-maker!'

'Can't I see him for a minute?'

I must have looked upset because the sergeant on duty took pity on me.

'All right . . . seeing as it's you we'll bring him in.' A few minutes later he came in between two real giants. They were both armed and their chinstraps were adjusted with absolute precision. Albert, who, in his misfortune, seemed to me more handsome than ever, took no notice of me but went over to the sergeant.

'How long d'you think I'll get Sarge?'

'We'll know tomorrow. With your record you'll be lucky if they let you off with three weeks.'

Albert grunted and then deigned to acknowledge my presence.

'Hello then! You here? I didn't expect you to turn up. What do you want?'

It was not quite the sort of reception I had anticipated as he must have seen from my expression, for his look softened and, resting his hand lightly on my shoulder, he began to comfort me with sweet, tender words.

When his term of punishment had ended, we met again. One night he got out over the wall to see me and began to talk of the future. The time came when I had to tell him that our plans must come to nothing; I could not make my life with him. As I had thought he would, he took it badly.

His last words to me that night were:

'I give you until tomorrow to reconsider.'

He wanted what was impossible. When I saw him the following day, I tried to make him understand. After listening to me without saying a word, he took my head in his hands, put his face very close to mine, and gave me a long searching look. Then, brusquely, he pushed me aside and stalked off; leaving me shattered . . . crying over a happiness I had lost almost before I had found it.

Three months later, Some of Albert's friends told me of his death in the Colonies.

This, then, was the little romance from which Raymond Asso created *Mon Légionnaire*.

There the story ended, but there was to be a sequel.

It happened many years later. I was no longer 'Miss Edith'. I was Piaf and I was appearing at the Folies-Belleville . . . an uncomfortable but friendly hall which, unhappily, has now been 'elevated' to cinema status and, like so many others, has lost all its character. I know Maurice Chevalier will agree with me for, as a boy, he often went there with his mother to see and cheer Mayol, Georgel and Polin.

But to return to my story. I was leaving the theatre one night with some friends, when a man in a cloth cap came up to me. He was quite well-dressed, youngish, spreading a bit round the middle, and had a somewhat bloated face.

He nodded to me without removing his cap.

'*B'jour!*'

A little startled, I replied with careful articulation: '*Bonjour, Monsieur!*'

He laughed. '*Monsieur,* is it? You don't recognize me . . . Albert of the Colonials?'

It was my Legionnaire; not dead at all . . . but how different from the man I had once known . . . and how much more different from the idealized image I had cherished over the years. Astounded, I stammered out something or the other.

'You've come a long way,' he said. 'You've been lucky . . done all right for yourself.'

I didn't know what to say to him. Fortunately he noticed my friends who were waiting discreetly a few yards away.

43

'I give you back to these gentlemen,' Albert said. 'It's been nice meeting you again.'

We parted.

The incident had saddened me and yet I was pleased because he appeared not to have identified himself as the man in the song which, by now, was well known. My true *légionnaire* ... the one I had loved ... he was dead!

Raymond Asso had written *Mon Légionnaire* for me; and Marguerite Monnot, whom I had introduced to Raymond, had written the music. It was my song, yet someone else launched it. The episode is worth relating if only to show that a discreditable action brings its own punishment. I had stolen *L'Etranger* from Annette Lajon ... someone stole *Mon Légionnaire* from me. Poetic justice!

One day I was dining with friends and someone mentioned Marie Dubas.

'I heard her yesterday at Bobino's, she has a really sensational song.'

'What's it called?'

'*Mon Légionnaire.*'

I jumped in my chair.

'But that's my song. I've been working at it for three weeks. If you think I'm going to ... ' I gulped down my coffee and hurried off to find Asso.

'What's this I hear? Have you given *Mon Légionnaire* to Marie Dubas?'

He protested: 'It's not true. Decruck must have thought that you didn't like it much and let her have it.'

Maurice Decruck was publishing the song. I rushed to his office to tell him exactly what I thought of him.

'Never!' he insisted. 'I have never shown it to Marie Dubas. It must be Marguerite Monnot!'

I ran to Margurite's.

'Not I!' she exclaimed. 'It was Asso!'

Closed circle! I never did find out how Marie had got hold of my song. Actually, I got my own back a little later when I 'stole' her *Flag of the Legion,* a song also composed by Raymond Asso and Marguerite Monnot:

> *Ah! là-là-là, la belle histoire,*
> *Y a trente gars dans le bastion,*
> *Torse nus, rêvant de bagarres,*
> *Ils ont du vin dans leurs bidons,*
> *Des vivres et des munitions.*
> *Ah! là-là-là, la belle histoire,*
> *Là-haut, sur les murs du bastion,*
> *Dans le soleil plane la Gloire*
> *Et dans le vent claque un fanion,*
> *C'est le fanion de la Légion!*

> *(Ah! là-là-là, what a fine story,*
> *Thirty fine lads in the fort,*
> *Stripped to the waist, dreaming of brawls;*
> *They've got their rations, their ammo,*
>   *and wine in their flasks.*
> *Ah! là-là-là, what a fine story,*
> *Up there on the walls of the fort,*
> *An aura of Glory in the hot sun,*
> *A flag snapping in the wind.*
> *It is the Standard of the Legion.)*

Marie Dubas once reproached me for taking this song. I reminded her that we were now even, and we became friends. I owe much to Marie Dubas, as I have often admitted. I modelled myself on her and it was by watching her that I learned so much. I must go back to the time I was singing at Gerny's. I had been there about a year, spoiled by Leplée, pampered and fêted by the regulars of the club. I had a very high opinion of myself, perhaps with good reason; the wonderful fairy-tale life had gone to my head. I was absolutely unbearable.

When, later on, Mitty Goldin was unwilling to give me a contract to sing at the A.B.C., it was because he still remembered our first meeting. I had an appointment to see him at four o'clock one afternoon. I arrived forty-five minutes late and somewhat prematurely played the part of a 'star'... demanding a fantastic fee with top billing and a programme with a minimum of twelve songs, among other things. I had been in the profession just eighteen months.

One day Raymond Asso took me to the A.B.C. to hear Marie Dubas sing. He had a definite motive for doing so, as I discovered after the show.

Marie Dubas was the star of the evening. She came on stage, vivacious, spritely, smiling, adorable in her white dress. It did not take me long to realize that here was a real artiste. Her versatility was staggering. With disconcerting ease she turned from comedy to drama and from tragedy to buffoonery. Movingly human in *Charlotte's Prayer*, she was irresistibly amusing in *Pedro*. Throughout she held the audience spellbound. Wheresoever she led, they followed willingly.

Gradually, in spite of my ignorance of the art of presentation, I began to see that in this magnificent performance nothing was left to chance; nothing was improvised. Facial expression, gestures, pose, intonation, all were carefully planned. Like a woman who wants to be beautiful for the man she loves, Marie wanted to be perfect for her audience.

Then it was over. Moist-eyed, dumbstruck by this great revelation, I did not even think to applaud her. As in a dream, I heard Raymond Asso's voice:

'*Now* do you know what an artiste is?'

For two weeks I went to every single performance; it was the best course of instruction anyone could have had. My admiration for Marie Dubas remains undiminished; to me she will always be 'The Great Marie'. A few years ago I met her in Metz where we were both appearing, although not at the same theatre. As she talked she noticed that I was politely addressing her as *'vous'*.

'Why don't you call me *"tu"*, Edith?' she said.

'No, Marie,' I answered. 'I admire you far too much. I am afraid it would spoil things ...'

Five

Papa, c était un lapin
Qui s'app'lait J.–B. Chopin
Et qu'avait son domicile
A Belleville ...

BRUANT

A few years ago on my way home to Paris, I stopped for lunch at Brive-la-Gaillarde. The owner of the restaurant, a garrulous sexagenarian, blooming with health, welcomed me like an old friend. I couldn't think who he was; so he explained that he had been head-waiter at Liberty's, the well-known cabaret in the place Blanche and he had seen me there 'just after the war'... not the last one but the 1914-18 war.

I made a rapid calculation ... at the time he claimed to have seen me, I could not have been more than five or six years old. He was obviously confusing me *La Môme Moineau*, known today as Mme Benitez-Reixach. I have mentioned this episode because I dislike being taken for *twice* my age; I am not so old that I have to be evasive about my years.

I was born on the 19th December 1915, at five o'clock in the morning, in Paris, at 72 rue de Belleville, or, to be precise, outside 72.

My father had gone out to call an ambulance, when my mother, knowing from her pains that the event was imminent, went to the front door to look for him. By the time the ambulance arrived I had already arrived in this world.

There was no midwife, in the normal sense of the word, but two policemen who, hearing my mother's groans, took charge and handled the situation very capably. It was quite an exceptional start in life.

I was given two names: Giovanna, which I have never liked, and Edith . . . Edith after the heroic English nurse Cavell who had recently been shot by the Germans in Belgium.

My mother was known as Line Marsa, but her real name was Maillard. She had show-business in her blood; her parents had roamed Algeria with their small travelling circus. My mother had come to Paris hoping to make her name as a singer but she never progressed beyond singing in cafés. I have always believed that she failed not through any lack of talent, but because luck was not on her side, and that Fate, in atonement, led me to the career of which she had dreamed.

My father, Louis Gassion, was an acrobat. Remarkably gifted athletically, extraordinarily supple and agile, he worked in circuses and market-places. He was fundamentally bohemian and preferred to work in the open . . . detesting any form of routine or regulation. He loved life and held that only those who are truly independent can enjoy it to the full. He was his own master, went freely wheresoever his fancy led him, and took orders from no one. Performing on some pavement, in a café or an army mess-hall, he felt free and happy. And he was far from being stupid . . . .

My mother had left him shortly after my birth and he was obliged to leave me in the care of my two grandmothers who lived in the provinces and who took turns at bringing me up. When I was seven I began to share his vagabond existence.

He had just signed up with the Caroli circus which was touring Belgium. We lived in a caravan and I did the chores. My days started early and the work was hard, but this sort of life with its constantly-changing horizons fascinated me. I discovered the enchantment of the sawdust ring with its fanfares, the sparkling costumes of the clowns, the gold-braided, red tunics of the lion tamers.

It could not last, of course. My father quarrelled with Caroli and went back to his beloved freedom. We returned to France, still travelling; but now we lived in hotels instead of the caravan. Father was once more his own boss . . . and mine too.

Father's act was fairly standard. He spread his canvas on the ground, ran through his introductory patter, before commencing his contortionist routine. His performance with a little more attention to presentation would not have been out of place in the arena of Medrano's. Afterwards my father would point at me and announce:

'Now this child is going to pass the hat round, and afterwards, to show her appreciation of your generosity, she will execute her perilous somersault.'

Then I would make a collection . . . but never the somersault.

One day, at Forges-les-Eaux, a disgruntled onlooker protested. He was quickly backed up by others who were already regretting the *sous* they had given to these *saltimbanques* who failed to keep their promises. But my father, never short of an answer, explained that I was recovering from a bout of 'flu and was still very weak.

'Surely,' he said, 'You do not expect the child to break her neck just to entertain you! However, since, by force of habit, I have mistakenly announced a feat that she can usually do with her eyes shut but which she is at present too weak to attempt, she will make amends by singing to you.'

I had never sung in my life and the only thing I knew was *La Marseillaise* . . . refrain only. In my frail, high-pitched voice, I did my best and the audience, touched, applauded. Acting on a surreptitious wink from my father, I passed the hat round a second time. Double returns . . . money for old rope!

My father was not a man to fail to learn from such an experience. Hardly was our canvas folded when he told me that in future I should sing at the end of each performance, and that same evening he had me learning *Nuits de Chine, Voici mon coeur,* and several others which were to constitute my first répertoire.

Papa Gassion was not exactly a tender man and I got more than my share of blows; but I survived. For a long time I thought that father did not love me. I was wrong. I realized this for the first time when I was about nine years old. We were in Lens, waiting for a tram. I was sitting on a suitcase gazing longingly in a toy-shop window. There was a doll . . . a rich child's doll . . . with blonde hair and a pale blue dress, with little hands that reached out to me. Never had I seen anything quite so beautiful!

Papa was smoking a cigarette at the kerb-side.

'What are you looking at?' he asked.

'A doll.'

'How much?'

'Five francs fifty.'

He put his hand in his pocket and brought out his worldly wealth . . . a grand total of six francs. Oh well, that was it! We had to eat and pay the hotel bill. We hadn't done any work that day and we couldn't be certain of making any money. The tram pulled in; I gave one last farewell glance at the doll.

Papa bought the doll for me the next day, before we moved on to another town, and then I knew that, in his own way, he loved me.

He kissed me only twice in my life.

The first time was when, at the age of nine, I was booked to appear at a small cinema. I had been in bed all day with a heavy cold and a sore throat, and my father had warned the management not to count on me. Towards evening I declared that ill or not I intended to appear. Papa told me that I was mad and that he had no wish to have my death on his conscience. But I was stubborn and, arguing that in our position, money, however little, was worth an effort, I overcame his objections. I sang, and when it was over Papa gave me two big kisses on the cheek. I was startled and happy. He had never been so proud of his daughter.

Quite a few years passed before he kissed me again. We had quarrelled some months earlier; like him I wanted freedom; I had to live my own life. I was now at Tenon where I had just brought my daughter Marcelle into the world. Father was my first visitor. He had heard that he was a grandfather and, forgetting our quarrel, he came rushing to see 'the little mother'. He stood silent for several minutes, then, with glistening eyes, he stooped to kiss me. The following day, my current 'step-mother' brought me a layette . . . nothing very splendid but nevertheless something for the baby to wear.

I must explain my use of the term 'current' step-mother.

My father was a handsome man and a fickle one; a bit of a womanizer . . . and he was never alone for very long. Sometimes he would be asked:

'Has that kid got a mother?' to which his reply was invariably:

'Rather more than she needs!'

Of my many more-or-less temporary 'step-mothers', some were kind and others less so; but none of them made me suffer, for Papa would not have tolerated that.

He would never consent to being separated from me although the opportunity arose advantageously many times. People would come forward and offer to take care of my education and to make sure that my artistic career was not neglected. He used to hear them out and then give a blank refusal, politely or otherwise, according to his mood.

On one occasion, in Sens, a very respectable couple offered to buy me for 100,000 francs cash ... quite a sum for that time ... but he refused outright.

'If you want a kid,' he said, 'Why don't you make your own? It's dead easy!'

One day, at a café in the Faubourg Saint-Martin ... I think it must have been Batifol's, where the variety artists meet for an apéritif ... a lady asked me to kiss her.

'My Daddy,' I said, 'does not allow me to kiss strangers.'

Papa was standing at the bar.

'You have my permission this time,' he said with a half-smile. 'She is your mother.' And then he added:

'The real one!'

My parents, who spent so little time together when they were alive, are buried together at the *Père-Lachaise* cemetery in Paris. It is with great tenderness that I remember them and I often pray by their grave.

I am sad when I recall my father's last hours. He had always been so care-free; yet now he turned his shrunken face towards me and said in a voice which was no longer of this world:

'Buy land, Edith; with a good farm you can be certain of never starving!'

Six

Quand il me prend dans ses bras,
Il me parle tout bas,
Je vois la vie en rose.
Il me dit des mots d'amour,
Des mots de tous les jours,
Ca me fait quelque chose.
Il est entré dans mon cœur,
Une part de bonheur
Dont je connais la cause . . . .

Of all professions, surely singing is the most wonderful. I doubt if there exists a more intense joy than that experienced by a singer when she passes to her audience a little of her personal richness.

Whenever I am asked the secret of success as a singer, I reply . . . with no claim to originality . . . 'Work, work, and more work'.

But there is more to it than that; it is necessary to be oneself . . . to retain one's own personality. This is not to say that others should be ignored; on the contrary, there is much to be learned by watching and studying others. In every singing performance there is a lesson, even if only in what not to do! It is always a temptation to speed on success, by becoming facile, by making certain 'concessions' to the audience; but this is something which must be avoided. When I am singing I give everything I have, and my whole being wills to establish contact with my audience; but if I fail to hold them, I do not and will not resort to stratagem, for this would diminish my worth, first of all in my own eyes and gradually in theirs also. I am against the intimate wink and the other gimmicks which buy applause.

It pays not to compromise. At Bobino's, when I sang *Mariage,* a song written by Henri Contet and Marguerite Monnot, I was given a very cool reception. But I persisted. I sang *Mariage* each time I appeared and eventually I made it a hit. I could mention other songs which, although good, were not at first successful and only became popular because I persevered with them.

I am very fastidious in selecting songs for my répertoire. Those which do not appeal to me I reject; but I will persist with those I like. I do not believe in having two répertoires . . . one for the stage and another for radio. To me, if a song is intrinsically good it can be sung anywhere.

Many manuscripts are submitted to me; some excellent, others execrable. Some are simply clumsy verses with poorly developed ideas, whilst others, too clever, are hashes of songs I have already sung (I have been offered no less than twenty adaptations of *Mon Légionnaire* and about the same number of *L'Accordéoniste*).

I retain only those with originality, sincerity, and meaning. I do not stick to one particular style in my programmes; variety is essential. Of course, I would not sing the amusing *Corrèque et réguyer* that I sang in my first appearance at the A.B.C. but whilst I do try to create an atmosphere of unity in my act, I also endeavour to introduce contrasts. Everyone will agree that *Jézebel* and *La vie en Rose* are completely different as are *L'Homme à la moto* and *Enfin le printemps, L'autre côté de la rue* and *Monsieur Saint-Pierre.*

My first concern is with the words of a song. I have never been able to understand the classic statement of Thérésa, the famous singer of the end of the last century. Her instruction to her song-writers was: 'Pretend to be stupid. If your verses are too clever, what is there left for me to do?'. Curious reasoning! To sing is to bring to life; impossible if the words are mediocre, however good the music.

The preceding paragraph might lead to the erroneous impression that I give secondary importance to the music. Without the music, a song might still be a very beautiful poem, but it certainly does not gain by such amputation.

Some years ago, Raymond Asso 'recited' his songs in cabaret. In spite of the poetic flawlessness of his verses and in spite of his undoubtedly considerable skill in speaking them, much of the emotional content was lacking. They needed music.... 'That music which ... the phrase is Raymond Asso's own ... gives a poem its true climate, its indispensable atmosphere'.

It would be impossible for me to speak of music without paying homage to the woman who is, I believe, the living incarnation of the art ... Marguerite Monnot, my best friend and the woman whom, of all others, I most admire.

Very pretty, refined and well-educated, she has but one handicap ... she seems to be so completely disinterested in publicity that one often feels that she requires some one to look after her business interests.

When she was three and a half, Marguerite was playing Mozart at the *Salle des Agriculteurs* ... her first payment was a soft toy cat. She was practically weaned on classical music and studied under Nadia Boulanger and Cortot. But she gave up a brilliant career as a concert pianist to write music for *chansons*. Her very first song was a waltz composed around the words of Tristan Bernard. It was called *Ah! les jolis mots d'amour* and Claude Dauphin and Alice Tissot hummed the tune in a film. The composition of *L'Etranger* marks her true début in an art in which she excels although her classical training was hardly an ideal preparation. It was followed by the music for *Mon Légionnaire* which she composed in a matter of hours and which brought her fame. And then all the others ... *Le Fanion de la Légion* and *Je n'en connais pas la fin* (with Raymond Asso); *Escale* (with Jean Marèze); *Histoire de Cœur, Le Ciel est fermé* and *Le Petit Homme* (with Henri Contet) and *La Goualante du Pauvre Jean* (with René Rouzaud). Because I am very proud of having myself collaborated with Marguerite, I must add to this far-from-complete list the following titles: *La Petite Marie, Le Diable est près de moi* and *Hymne à l'amour* ... just three of the songs we created together.

No other woman can boast of having so many of her compositions sung throughout the world. Her success is well merited.

I have been lucky enough to be the first to sing many beautiful songs; but there are many, too, that I would have been glad to introduce yet which I know I shall never sing. For example, there is Louis Aubert's *La Mauvaise Prière*. Damia really *lives* this outstanding song with the deep dramatic intensity of which she is capable, and each time I hear her I receive a new emotional shock. Each time. I have applauded and cried out my admiration for her, and then returned home depressed; for no matter how much I long to sing this song, how could I even attempt it after hearing Damia!

I have already mentioned my esteem for the talent of Marie Dubas. More than once she has made me cry with *La Prière de la Charlotte*. It is the story of a pitiful little waif who, one Christmas Day, cold and hungry, begs the Holy Virgin to let her die after first offering to relieve her for a while of her precious burden, for ....

Un enfant, c'est lourd à la fin . . . .

(A child becomes heavy after so long . . . .)

I know the words . . . those moving, pathetic, *human* words . . . so well; but I shall never sing them. To try to follow Marie Dubas would be too great a risk to take.

I have sung *Comme un Moineau* although it was never mine. It was excusable because I was only fifteen at the time and had never even heard the name Fréhel.[1] I met her years later at Leplée's. The song was still a part of her répertoire and when I heard her sing it I was quite ashamed, and I understood that I had much to learn before I could call myself an *artiste*.

Many other titles come to mind of songs I wish had been mine: *Je chante,* for example, written by Charles Trenet; Yves Montand's great success *Les Premiers Pas; La Guadeloupe,* which bears the brand of Marie Dubas; *Miss Otis regrette,* which Jean Sablon sang so well; and, of course, *La Vie en Rose!*

I wrote the words and music of *La Vie en Rose* myself in 1945, but I was not the one to introduce it. I had already composed the music for several songs, including *Jour de Fête,* all of which had been arranged by Marguerite Monnot; but I was not yet a member of *S.A.C.E.M.*[2] (Here I must digress for a moment because I know that some of my colleagues, when they read these words, will exclaim 'Has she forgotten that she failed her entrance exam?' So I shall forestall them. I confess. I *did* fail it. I could mention that at the time I was in very poor health, but why should I look for excuses? Anyway, I got through eight months later and when Marguerite Monnot told me that she herself had failed the first time, as had Christiné, the composer

---

[1] Fréhel: a *Chanteuse* who was at the height of her fame during the period between the two wars.

[2] *S.A.C.E.M. La Société des Auteurs, Compositeurs et Editeurs de Musique.*

of *Phi-Phi,* I was consoled.)

To get back to the story of *La Vie en Rose.* One afternoon in May, 1945, I was sitting in a café on the Champs-Elysées drinking port with my friend Marianne Michel. Marianne had come from Marseille. She had made a promising start in Paris and was looking for the song which would make her name.

'Why don't you write one for me,' she said.

I had already written the music for *La Vie en Rose.* I hummed it to her and, finding it pleasing, she asked me to finish it. There were no words and it lacked a title.

'All right!' I said, 'I'll do it this minute.'

I took my pen and wrote two lines on the table-cloth.

> *Quand il me prend dans ses bras,*
> *Je vois les choses en rose . . .*

> (When he takes me in his arms,
> Things take on a rosy hue . . .)

Marianne said:

'You think that's right . . . "things"? Why not "Life"?'

'Good idea! And that gives us a title . . . your title . . . *La Vie en Rose.*'

I finished the song but, since I was not a member of the *S.A.C.E.M.,* I needed someone to sign it. I showed it to Marguerite Monnot who looked at me, amazed.

'Surely you're not going to sing junk like this!' she exclaimed.

'I was relying on getting your signature.'

'No? Well, I can't say I'm very keen.'

I did not insist. I took the manuscript away and approached other composers. They too refused, and there was even one who said:

'You must be joking! You've refused to sing ten of my songs in three years and yet you expect me to assume responsibility for something you are not going to sing yourself and which will certainly be a flop. You're asking too much!'

I began to think I would never get the required signature. But then Louiguy, who later wrote *Bravo pour le Clown* for me, came to my aid and signed. I am quite sure he has never had cause to regret his action.

And so *La Vie en Rose* was launched by Marianne Michel and has become a world-wide success. Translated into about a dozen languages, including Japanese, it has been recorded innumerable times by artists such as Bing Crosby and Louis Armstrong and the sale of records reached the fabulous figure of three million. It is no less popular in the United States than in France and each time I sing in New York the audience calls for it. People hum the tune on the streets, and on Broadway there is a night-club called *La Vie en Rose* ... probably the only one in the world to be named after a French song.

I did not sing this song until two years after Marianne. I am happy to have written it for her, but I shall always regret the fact that it was not mine from the start.

Seven

Depuis quelque temps l'on fredonne
Dans mon quartier une chanson,
La musique en est monotone
Et les paroles sans façon.
Ce n'est qu'une chanson des rues,
Dont on ne connaît pas l'auteur,
Depuis que je l'ai entendue,
Elle chante et danse en mon cœur ....

For several years I sang only the songs that Raymond Asso wrote for me. His refrains were popular from the very first time they were heard, and they are not dated. If, tomorrow, a star singer were to re-introduce them, they would be as popular as ever and all France would be humming them; songs like: *Je n'en connais pas la fin, Le Grand Voyage du pauvre nègre, C'est lui que mon cœur a choisi, Browning* and *Paris-Méditerranée* which, like *Mon Légionnaire*, found its inspiration in one of my personal recollections.

I was travelling to the south of France by an over-night train, and I fell asleep with my head on the shoulder of a handsome man whom chance had given me as travelling companion. His cheek had rested very softly against mine and I had not pushed him away.

Un train dans la nuit vous emporte,
Derrière soi des amours mortes
Et dans le cœur un vague ennui ....

Alors sa main a pris la mienne
Et j'avais peur que le jour vienne.
J'étais si bien contre lui.

(A train carries me through the night,
Leaving behind those dead loves,
And there is a sort of emptiness in the heart.
Then his hand took mine
And I began to dread the coming dawn.
I was so happy to be close to him.)

At Marseille, on the platform of the Saint-Charles Station, two police inspectors were waiting for him. He saw them too late to escape and my last glimpse of him was as he was being led, handcuffed, away through the crowd towards the station-exit. I never heard of him again and it is probable that, like the *légionnaire,* he does not suspect that he inspired one of Raymond Asso's most beautiful songs.

When the war separated me from Raymond, I had to find other song-writers. He was not easy to replace; although thousands of new songs are born each year, good writers, as I have said before, are rare. Béranger[1] put it in a nutshell when he wrote:

Without trying to exaggerate my own small merit . . . . indeed, one would have to be pretty smart to discover variety in my work . . . I know, as every-one knows, that there are more good dramatic authors to be found than good song-writers.

This fact is as true today as it was then, as I have good reason to know. Happily, on several occasions during my often disappointing quest for writers, fortune was willing to smile on me. I did not, for instance, have to search for Michel Emer; he came to me. The story is sufficiently out of the ordinary to be worth the telling.

[1] Beranger: a poet and song-writer at the time of the French Restoration.

I had bumped into him before the war in the corridors of Radio-Cité and had found him a sympathetic man with intelligent eyes behind huge glasses, a broad smile that revealed his gleaming teeth, scintillating conversation and, moreover, the kind of courteousness that is not over-common in the studios of radio and cinema. I knew that he had talent but, to me, Michel Emer represented the flowers, the blue skies, the little birds . . . a sort of latter-day Delmet, writing some quite pretty pieces but certainly nothing suitable for me.

We had been at war some forty-eight hours. At my home on the avenue Marceau I was told that Michel Emer was waiting outside with a song he wanted me to try out. I sent a message saying that I had a rehearsal and could not see him, but he insisted. He had just been called up, it appeared, and would be catching the midnight train from Gare de l'Est to join his unit. I simply must hear his song before he left. I decided to humour him and when he came in I warned him:

'I give you ten minutes, Corporal Emer.'

'More than enough,' he replied, and sitting himself at the piano, he began to play *L'Accordéoniste*.

> *La fill' de joie est belle*
> *Au coin d'la rue là-bas.*
> *Elle a un' clientèle*
> *Qui lui remplit son bas . . . .*

> (Down there on the corner
> stands a beautiful little wanton
> whose customers are making her rich . . . .

An excellent pianist, he sang badly; but I listened with bated breath. Before he had begun the second verse, I had already made up my mind . . . I was determined to be the first to sing this song that I had almost refused to hear.

Elle écout' la java,
Mais ell' ne la dans' pas,
Ell' ne regarde mêm' pas la piste,
Mais ses yeux amoureux
Suivent le jeu nerveux
Et les doigts secs et longs de l'artiste . . . .

(She listens to the Java,
But she doesn't dance,
She doesn't even watch the others,
Her loving eyes
Follow the nervous movements
Of the accordeonist's long, bony fingers.)

And then, right at the end, after the last line of the third verse, comes a veritable stroke of genius. The music continues for a moment until suddenly the girl, overcome with emotion and unable to bear it any longer, cries out:

Arrêtez! Arrêtez la musique!

(Stop! Stop the music!)

Michel did not get a chance to ask me what I thought of the song.

'Again!' I said, and he played it a second, and then a third time.

On and on we went. He had arrived at two o'clock in the afternoon and I did not let him go until five o'clock the next morning. I made him stay because I had decided to sing the song that very night at Bobino's; so he stayed for the *Première* and was three hours late in reporting to his unit. He narrowly missed being court-martialled, but he was happy in spite of the luke-warm reception the public gave his composition. The audience seemed unable to decide whether or not the song was finished. However,

L'Accordéoniste was to prove itself before very long.

A writer of lyrics and a composer of music, Michel Emer has the gift, rarer than one might think, of finding melodies which stick in the mind from the first time of hearing.

I have already spoken of the importance of the words, but a song is no less a melody. 'If a song has no melody,' writes Jean Wiener, the author of *Grisbi,* 'it is not quite a song.' And he goes on to define the word 'melody'. It is 'tuneful, simple, symetrical, logical, constant, accessible, and such that it tends to impress itself on the memory.'

Melodies like this, Michel Emer produces like an apple tree produces apples. People are sometimes disconcerted by the audacity of his compositions but they invariably end by accepting them, and I always feel quite secure when I sing one the songs he has written for me: *Monsieur Lenoble, Télégram, Qu'as-tu fait, John?, Le Disque Use,* and the others, not forgetting *De l'autr' côté d'la Rue:*

> *Y a pas à dire, elle aim' trop la vie*
> *Et un peu trop les beaux garçons.*
> *Elle a un cœur qui s'multiplie.*
> *Et ça lui fait d'droles d'additions!*

> (You can't deny she loves life too much,
> and she's a bit too fond of the lads.
> She can multiply her heart . . .
> Which brings her some peculiar additions . . . .)

I got to know Henri Contet at the studio where, in 1941, we were shooting *Montmartre-sur-Seine.* He was a journalist and had been put in charge of the publicity for the film.

One day in the canteen he told me that some ten years earlier he had 'perpetrated' some songs.

'I was only twenty,' he added in justification.

One of the songs, *Traversée,* written around a melody

by Jacques Simonot, had found favour with Lucienne Boyer and she had included it in her programme, even though it was an extremely dramatic piece and not at all in keeping with her usual style. But the critics, who have a taste for 'classification' and who have no love for any departure from the norm, took it upon themselves to remind Lucienne that her speciality was 'charm' and that she should stick to it. And so she dropped *Traversée* and Henri Contet, fed-up, gave up song-writing.

But he went on writing poems. I read some of them and enthusiastically demanded that he write a song for me. Shortly after, he brought me two: *Le Brun et le Blond,* and *C'était une histoire d'amour.* My hunch had not failed me . . . Henri Contet had a fine career as a song-writer before him.

He followed the road, and has not yet reached the end. I am indebted to him for many songs which are among the most beautiful in my répertoire. There is, for instance, *Le Vagabond:*

> *C'est un vagabond*
> *Qui est joli garçon.*
> *Il chant' des chansons*
> *Qui donnent le frisson.*

> (Just a vagabond,
> A handsome lad
> Whose songs
> Send a shiver up your spine.)

And then *Un air d'accordéon, Y a pas d'Printemps,* which he wrote in twenty-five minutes following a bet I made with him . . . and which he won . . . *Coup de Grisou, Monsieur Saint-Pierre, Histoire de Cœur, Mariage, Le Petit Homme,* which, with wonderful simplicity, described

66

the solitude of man in present-day environment, and, also, *Bravo Pour le Clown* ... a song that I would certainly not want to forget:

> *Je suis Roi, et je règne,*
> *Bravo, bravo!*
> *J'ai fait mon numéro*
> *Bravo bravo!*
> *Venez, que l'on m'acclame,*
> *J'ai fait mon numéro*
> *Tout en jetant ma femme*
> *Du haut du chapiteau ... :*

> (I am King, and I reign,
> Bravo, bravo!
> My laughs come straight from a bleeding heart,
> Bravo, bravo!
> Come! How I am acclaimed,
> I have done my turn,
> And thrown my wife from the top of the tent.)

Henri Contet, whom I believe to be a great poet ... and I am not alone in this opinion ... continues to write his verses. Mary Marquet has, on several occasions, during his poetry recitals, praised him in similar vein, and that, in itself, is a commendation. I hope that one day he will please his friends and astonish those who do not yet know of him, by publishing all his poems in one volume ... and I also hope he will go on writing fine songs for me to sing.

Eight

Il a des yeux,
C'est merveilleux,
Et puis des mains,
Pour des matins,
Il a des rires
Pour me séduire
Et des chansons . . . .

The first time I heard Yves Montand sing was at the Moulin Rouge. I had a fourteen-day contract there, and the management of this famous music-hall in place Blanche had invited me to choose the *vedette américaine*[1] for the programme of which I was the big name.

I thought first of the versatile Roger Dann who was then dividing his time between singing tours and operetta; but he was not free. Then someone suggested Yves Montand. I had met him once, years earlier, in Marseille where he was taking his first steps in the profession under the guidance of the late Emile Audiffred; and of course I had heard much about him. He had a large following in the south and he was well known for the 'bloomers' he made each time he appeared at L'Alcazar in Marseille . . . the oldest French music-hall, built in 1852.

He made his Paris *début* in 1944 at the A.B.C. . . . the occasion was not far short of being disastrous.

Half-dead with stage-fright, and wearing a most eccen-

---

[1] Vedette américane: American Star; the name given to the performer appearing immediately before the first interval.

tric check jacket, he faced his audience. Some wag in the gallery shouted 'Zazou!'[1] and the hall, stuffed with the followers of Dassary, star of the show, burst into laughter. Not much of a beginning! His diction was, at that time, still on the rough side and his Marseille accent gave a peculiar sound to his 'o's', especially in the word 'harmonica' which occurred frequently in his songs. All this, combined with his excessive gestures, did little to help him and this first evening was hardly a triumphant success. But he was very quick to learn from the adventure, and the next evening, leaving his frightful jacket in the dressing-room, he went on stage wearing brown trousers and in his shirt-sleeves, collar unbuttoned and chest half-exposed. He was a hit!

One can, *a priori,* have confidence in him. When an artiste is willing to correct his own faults; if he re-adjusts his aim when necessary; then you can back him to win ... he is not likely to fall by the wayside.

And now it was suggested that he appear in my programme at the Moulin Rouge. Emile Audiffred asserted that 'his boy' had come a long way since his *début* at the A.B.C. and I agreed, in principle, to his being offered a contract ... subject to a satisfactory audition. Yves has since confessed to me that at the time he thought I was being most unreasonable; he had, in fact, confided to his manager that I was, in his opinion, a 'merchant of gloom', like all the *réalistes,* and an *'enquiquineuse'*[2] into the bargain.

The day of the audition came round and I sat almost alone and lost in the shadow of the vast auditorium of the Moulin. Yves began to sing and immediately held me. His personality was terrific, giving the impression of strength and solidity. His hands were eloquent, powerful, sensitive;

---

[1] Zazou: derogatory epithet for person adopting snazzy or 'spivvy' dress.

[2] Enquiquineuse: a damned nuisance or frightful bore.

his face handsome and tormented; and in his deep voice there was miraculously, no trace of the Marseille accent. Patiently, calculatingly, he had rid himself of it.

He now needed only one thing . . . some songs. Those he sang were frankly impossible: cowboy refrains . . . simple and sometimes vulgar . . . a sort of pseudo-Americanism used for effect and because the Liberation was not far off. I thought they were quite dreadful; I was sure Yves Montand was worth more than that.

When he had finished his fourth song, I left my seat and went to the front of the hall. He stepped forward to the edge of the stage. I shall always be able to picture myself, small, as I am, completely overshadowed by this tall young man and looking up at him from the level of his ankles.

I told him that I thought he was great; that he was obviously destined to go to the top. Then I joined him on the stage and gave him my opinion of his répertoire. We must, I said, change it completely. He should concentrate on works of quality; songs that he could bring to life; songs that would enable him to express something.

He looked at me in astonishment, thinking, probably, that I was poking my nose into what did not concern me. He eventually replied with a rather unconvinced 'yes'. This, clearly, in no way implied agreement with me, and was said simply to avoid trouble. He did not want to oppose the star of the show but, at the same time, he was not really interested in her advice.

I asked him if he had ever heard me sing, and when he replied in the negative, I said:

'Eh bien! Now it's my turn. Seize the opportunity!'

He went down and took a seat near where I had sat. I rehearsed my programme.

When I had finished, he climbed on to the stage and came up to me; and having praised me in such a manner that I prefer not to enlarge on it, he said simply:

'As to my répertoire, you are quite right. I shall do as you say although it's going to be hard!'

Today, Yves Montand is one of the greatest singers of the song-world. By degrees, yet swiftly, he has avoided the style that threatened to hold him prisoner. Jean Guigo and Henri Contet gave him *Battling Joë*, *Luna-Park* and *Gilet Rayé*, first-class songs of which he can be proud. In them, Yves made the characters live, in an unforgettable way: the unhappy boxer who becomes blind in *Battling Joë*, for example:

> *C'est un nom maint'nant oublié,*
> *Une pauvre silhouett' qui penche,*
> *Appuyée sur une cann' blanche . . . .*

> (A name now forgotten,
> Just a poor stooping shadow
> Leaning on a white stick . . . .)

Or the little bourgeois of *Ce Monsieur-là*, for whom suicide is the only way out; and then again, the inn-keeper in *Gilet Rayé* who ends up as a convict. Innumerable others have followed and it would be impossible to name all the songs which he has introduced and stamped with his strong personality.

Yves Montand has won his fight.

He has won by virtue of his courage and determination for, although he changed his style over-night, he had a long, hard struggle to win acceptance of the 'new' Montand. He changed his skin, but the public had grown used to his old ways and, like the critic, it does not take kindly to changes in routine. In Lyon and in Marseille, audiences which had previously acclaimed him now greeted him with reserve. He could have regained favour by going back to his old popular style; but he refused to do so. He had chosen his path and would not retrace his footsteps, however great the temptation. He knew that the new songs were good, and he was going to stick with them.

At times there was really a battle beween Yves and a restive audience. He would leave the stage worn-out, discontented even angry . . . but never beaten.

Time and time again he has said to me:

'It's dreadful, Edith, but I won't give in. I know I'm right· They'll have to admit it eventually.'

And then one day, at the Etoile, in 1945 . . . once again he was the *vedette américaine* in a show of which I was the star . . . acclaimed by an audience which really loved him, he came into the wings beaming:

'This is it, Edith,' he said, 'this time I really had them.'

A few years later he was back again in the same hall . . . this time with top billing . . . and again he was sensational. His youthful mastery was acknowledged and he became The Great Montand.

Our paths have separated now, but I shall always be proud of having played a part in his climb to fame.

I would like to mention now, something that Maurice Chevalier once said. It was on an occasion, some years ago, after a performance at either the Empire or the Alhambra. For the very first time he had had the whole of the second half of the show to himself, reaching, at last, the pinnacle of which he had dreamed since he was only *'le petit Chevalier'*, almost a quarter of a century before. His performance had ended with ovation after ovation, and innumerable friends and well-wishers had been unwilling to leave the theatre without having touched the hand of this conquering hero. He had received their congratulations with his customary imperturbability and affability and had then gone off to finish the evening with a few close friends.

'They are such a funny crowd,' he said. 'There are those

who say "Ah well, Old Chap it's taken you quite a while to get to the top", and there are those who say "It didn't take you long to get there". But have you noticed that it is the former whose manner is the friendlier? They are my pillars of strength, the ones who know that I've had to work for it . . . that I've had no presents from life.'

The observation is an accurate one. The public has a tendency to believe that our struggle for recognition begins when they hear of us for the first time. It never enters their heads that we might have been fighting for years before they even suspect that we exist. They seem to think, too, that we have succeeded only because good fortune happened to give us a nudge in the right direction.

For my part, I know that more than once I have been tempted to give up the battle. Often I have waited in the office of some impresario and eventually had to leave without having been seen. I am quite familiar with those long journeys . . . third class . . . to the depths of Brittany or Dauphiné to perform for a miserable little fee. I have had to work my way up from being 'first on' to occupying second, third and then fourth place on the bill. From there I progressed to *vedette américaine* and then the supreme reward . . . Top of the Bill. Difficult days indeed; but a most useful apprenticeship.

In music-hall, as elsewhere . . . and perhaps to an even greater degree than elsewhere . . . artistic mastery, the indispensable adjunct to talent, is not conjured up out of nothing; one has to acquire it gradually. This is a prime truth; but it is one which many of the young artistes of today seem to disregard. They want, as the saying goes, to arrive before they set out. With the help of radio and records, a clever agent who is not short of capital can make a star in a matter of months. And these young stars, hearing the repeated assertions of their genius, come to believe in it themselves, when, in fact, they have yet to learn, if not

73

all, at least the greater part of a difficult art of which they have not taken the trouble to learn the a b c.

Herein lies the explanation of why some of these 'stars' are no more than meteors, flashing briefly in the sky of the world of music-hall, only to vanish as quickly as they appeared.

Happily, there are also those youngsters, in great number, who work, and who seek; who, by dint of long and patient effort, in the manner of the 'old 'uns', eventually find themselves and gain in stature by their labours.

Today, as never before, the singing profession is rich with young original talent. I have had the happy opportunity of being able to help some of them to emerge and I hope to do so again in the future.

It is a great thing to know that one has brought happiness to someone.

Nine

Une cloche sonne, sonne,
Sa voix d'échos en échos
Dit au monde qui s'étonne:
'C'est pour Jean-François Nicot!'
C'est pour accueillir une âme,
Une fleur qui s'ouvre au jour,
A peine, à peine une flamme,
*   encore faible, qui réclame*
Protection, tendresse, amour!'

The mention of young singers leads me now to write of my friends *Les Compagnons de la Chanson*. There are nine of them, as you know, and the title of a film they once made proclaimed them as 'Nine Boys, One Heart'... to which I will add 'And the Talent of a Hundred'.

I first met them during the war when they appeared in a show at the Comédie-Francaise. This group of young singers used to specialize in folksong. The great stage personalities Marie Bell and Louis Seigner had heard them sing in Lyon and had had the happy notion of bringing them to Paris. On the night in question, the show was interrupted by an air-raid alert and the greater part of the audience decided to leave; but when the danger had passed, the show continued and I did not regret having stayed.

Les Compagnons were undoubtedly talented. They lacked experience and their style was somewhat camp-fire-ish, but if it sometimes happened that they failed to get the last ounce from their songs, it in no way lessened their appeal and charm. One did not have to be a crystal-gazer to know that they had great possibilities.

I chatted to them for a long time after the show. I took them home with me and we spent several enjoyable evenings singing to each other. And then, for a while, we lost touch. But in 1945 we were on tour together in Germany. We had the whole show to ourselves; they monopolizing the first half, and I the second. We became real friends.

It was because we were such friends that I was able, after hearing them sing many times, to speak freely of what was on my mind.

The old French folksongs they were singing, I told them, were proof of their own good taste. The arrangements were well-chosen, their presentation was excellent and the blending of the voices perfect; and yet I feared they were heading in the wrong direction. I am not carrying a torch for 'commercial' songs, I said, but if you really want to reach a bigger public and the record fans, you'll have to change your répertoire. I love the way you sing *Perrine était servante*. It's a lovely song, but you'll never hear people humming it in the street. What you need are tunes which will become popular ... tunes that stick in the memory; and, naturally, love-songs.

They listened to my little sermon politely, like well-mannered boys; they even had the courtesy to offer a few very small objections to my ideas ... and it was quite obvious that I had in no way convinced them. I did not insist; after all, they were their own masters and old enough to know what they wanted to make of themselves, since, between them, their ages totalled about two-hundred years ... say two hundred and ten for good measure.

However, as you have perhaps noticed, I am not one

76

to abandon my little ideas without a fight. I was to return to the charge a little later.

When 'Gilles' wrote the words and music of *Les Trois Cloches* (The Three Bells) he decided to sign it with his real name, Jean Villard. I don't blame him. I had heard him sing it himself at the Coup de Soleil, his own cabaret in Lausanne . . . a place, let me say in parenthesis, which has a part in the history of the war . . . and I had been absolutely dazzled by it. 'I'm going to sing you,' I thought, as I listened to the song.

But when Gilles gave me the song, I found myself in a siuation as new to me as it was unexpected; for, although I was still determined to sing it, I felt, for some reason, that I could not sing it alone . . . it needed different treatment. But what? It was difficult to say.

When the German tour was over I returned to Paris, with the score of *Les Trois Cloches* in my portfolio. The song was beginning to haunt me; there it was, a true masterpiece, lying dormant whilst some writers were making a fortune out of what can only be described as 'utter tripe'. The knowledge was sickening!

And then one day I was struck by an idea which should have come to me long before. The song, unsuitable as a solo work, was perfect for several voices. It was but a short step, or, rather, a short phone call, between this idea and an approach to Les Compagnons.

Their refusal was immediate and categorical. Sing that song? Not at any price!

I was disconcerted; but by no means defeated.

'How would it be if I sang it with you?' I asked.

I was trying this tack without any great hope . . . almost certain that they would reject the idea. Imagine my surprise when they agreed.

Together we worked on it. We decided on a spectacular presentation with orchestra and pipe-organ, and in the sonorous décor which added to its beauty, the work began to take on extraordinary breadth. And yet the public received it, at first, with some reserve. Perhaps they felt instinctively that Les Compagnons were not singing with their usual gusto ... that they took no pleasure in the presentation and were, possibly, singing it more as a favour to me than because they wanted to. If so, I am inclined to think they were right. Anyway, the song was certainly not the great success I had hoped it would be.

One day, at my request, Jean Cocteau came to listen to the songs that Les Compagnons and I had built up together, including, of course *Les Trois Cloches*. Modesty prevents me repeating the compliments Jean saw fit to heap upon us when we had finished. I will mention only his opinion of our blended voices. Together, he said, we formed a remarkably harmonious *ensemble*, and our interpretations stirred up a very pure and rare emotion. We had brought him almost to the point of tears, he added.

From that day, everything changed. Responding to the commendation of the poet, Les Compagnons began to sing *Les Trois Cloches* with as much conviction as I, and, suddenly, the song rocketed to the top. The last people to appreciate its value were the record companies who, with their usual dogmatic authority, asserted that it had no commercial worth; that it would fail to find a good market and did not justify the expense of cutting. Some shrewdness! Copies of the record sold by the thousand, in every country in the world, and sales reached record numbers ... a total of more than a million copies.

In the United States, where Jean-François Nicot became Jimmy Brown, sixty thousand records of *The Jimmy Brown Song,* as the American version was called, were sold in three weeks.

Les Compagnons, in spite of this, went on singing their old French folksongs; but, stubborn, and sure that I was right, I did not give up hope of persuading them to change completely one day. Surely they could not remain forever tied to a répertoire which prevented them from exploiting the full measure of their talent! It was simply a matter of finding the right song . . . the one that would bring them round to seeing things my way. This song, when it arrived, turned out to be *La Marie:*

> *T'en fais pas, la Marie, t'es jolie!*
> *Je r'viendrai,*
> *Nous aurons du bonheur plein la vie.*
> *T'en fais pas, la Marie!*

> (Don't worry, Marie, you're so pretty!
> I'll be back.
> We'll have a life full of happiness;
> Don't worry, Marie!)

André Grassi had written this song for me, but somehow I felt that it was more suitable for the group. I offered it to them but I cannot claim that it overwhelmed them. However, at my insistence, and with the success of *Les Trois Cloches* yet fresh in their memories, they agreed to attempt it. A few months later, *La Marie* won for them *Le Grand Prix du Disque.*

After this they began to modernize themselves. They adopted some of the songs of Charles Trenet and gradually became the group we know today. I do not regret having nudged them along the path of evolution; it would have been such a pity had they never sung *Moulin Rouge* by Jacques Larue and Georges Auric, or *Le petit Coquelicot* (Raymond Asso and Valéry), *C'était mon copain* (Louis Amade and Gilbert Bécaud), *Quand un soldat* (Francis Lemarque), or *La Prière* by Francis Jammes and Georges Brassens. How terrible, too, if *La Chanson du Célibataire, Le Violon de tante Estelle,* and

Le Cirque had never flowed from the pen of Jean Broussolle!

It was with Les Compagnons that I made my first trip to the United States. For some time I had wanted to join the ranks of the 'discoverers' of America, but I know now that I shoud have waited a little longer ... I should have known that a singing-tour in a foreign country is not a thing to be lightly undertaken ... especially in a country of which one does not speak the language. I should have realized the hazards awaiting me and fore-armed myself accordingly. I might then have avoided those errors for which I later committed.

We made the crossing by sea, and I must confess that when we entered Hudson Bay I was feeling uneasy. In one of those extraordinary pieces of literary compression of which he is so great an exponent, Jean Cocteau has written that 'New York is a town on end'. There could be no abler definition of the impression one gets when, from the deck of the liner gliding at the very foot of those structures which literally crush you with their fantastic size, this Brobdingnagian city bursts upon you. The scale is so far removed from our own that it is like entering a different universe. I felt even smaller than I really am and my first thought was, although I kept it to myself, 'Why the devil didn't you stay at home, Edith?'.

We opened in a place on Broadway's Forty-Eighth Street ... in the centre of the world of theatre and night-life. Our show was patterned on those which had brought us such success in France, and it soon became apparent that this was an error on our part. It clashed with American custom. I should have known that music-hall, such as we have in Paris, no longer exists in the U.S.A.; there is no equivalent of the A.B.C. and the Paladium on that side of the Atlantic. Singers and variety artistes are booked as 'added attractions' in cinemas, or they appear in night-clubs which put on big revues ... rather similar to the shows at the Lido or the Tabarin in Paris.

Although at the time my English was quite rudimentary, I had had two of my songs translated for the benefit of my audience. I did my best but the result was disappointing. The polite applause showed that my effort had been appreciated but it was obvious that they had not understood me. I assumed that my accent had been at fault. Any doubt I might have felt about this was completely banished when, after the show, a most courteous gentleman told me ... with no hint of sarcasm, I hasten to add ... that he had particularly enjoyed the songs I had sung *in Italian!*

With the intention of making my French songs 'less foreign', I had requested the compere to say a few words about each one before I sang it. This was another mistake. The introduction, however brief, was a hiatus which interfered with the *rapport* I had established with the audience. Not that there was much *rapport* anyway! As my name was announced, a quiver of anticipation would pass through the room already 'warmed-up' by Les Compagnons. Here she came; *Idiss* Piaf! ... a breath of Gay Paree! Hair-do by Antonio! Make-up by someone else! Evening-gown costing hundreds of thousands of *francs!*

And then I came on in my little black dress. What a picture!

And that was not all, for not only did I fail to come up to the American expectation of what a Parisienne should be, but also I sang songs which were not at all to their liking. They found that *L'Accordéoniste, Où sont-ils, tous mes copains?,* and the others I tried, lacked cheerfulness. They were more accustomed to those syrupy melodies where *amour* rhymes with *toujours* and, not quite as

81

bad, *tendresse* with *ivresse* and *caresse*. I must admit that at first their adverse reactions surprised and saddened me, but later, when I came to know the Americans better, I understood.

The day of an American is an exhausting one. He accepts this philosophically, but when it is over he wants to relax. He knows very well that there is a coarser side of life where rogues abound ... indeed; he has to deal with it every day ... but in the evening he wants to forget about it. His needs and tastes are simple and unsophisticated. Why, he asks himself, when he has deposited his cares in the cloak-room with his hat, does this little French woman have to sing her miserable songs about miserable people?

I had journeyed all the way to America only to fall flat on my face almost as soon as I got there. The knowledge of my failure came as a shock, of course, but it was not the first time I had had to surmount an obstacle. All that was needed was courage, a quality which, fortunately, I have never lacked.

Meanwhile, Les Compagnons had unleashed a storm of enthusiasm in that same public I had failed to move. Won over by the beauty of their voices as much as by their presentation and youthful vivacity, audience after audience acclaimed them; their press-reports were excellent ... mine never more than mediocre. It was time, I felt, for me to go home.

I told them of my decision. They did not need me, I said, and should only be a drag on them if I remained. It was best that we separate; they to continue the tour, and I to board the next boat for France. And had it not been for Virgil Thompson, this is what would have happened.

Virgil Thompson is a dramatic critic and it is rare for him to write about music-hall artists; even so he devoted a two-column article on the front page of one of the big New York dailies to me. It was just the encouragement I needed.

Since those days I have come to terms with America, and I can look back on the bad days with a certain amount of philosophy; but without any doubt my first contact with New York was disastrous and for the first time, perhaps, in my career, I really lost confidence. I had but one idea ... to get back to Paris; back to my friends and the audiences who appreciated me. Virgil Thompson's article restored my faith in myself for it's conclusion was to the effect that if the American public were to allow me to depart without having proved myself, it would thereby demonstrate its own incompetence and stupidity.

With this article in his brief-case, my American agent, Clifford Fischer, went off to see the directors of the Versailles, one of the most elegant cabarets of Manhattan, where he succeeded in obtaining a booking for me.

'When people get used to the little black dress, he told the directors, and when they realize that a Parisienne does not always appear in a plumed hat and a gown with a long train, they'll be fighting for a chance to hear Piaf sing. I am even willing,' he added, 'to make good any money you might lose on her.'

Clifford Fischer, who would certainly not have liked to pay out, was never called upon to keep his word. My English was improving, I cut out the compere's introduction of each song, and the public, fore-warned, now expected a singer and not a mannequin.

The battle had been won. I left the stage to a great ovation and, although my contract had been for one week only, I stayed at the Versailles for twelve consecutive weeks.

Since then I have been to the U.S.A. many times, singing not only at the Versailles but also in Hollywood, Miami, Boston and Washington, among others, until at last I reached the very peak . . . a recital at Carnegie Hall, the American Temple of Music. I am sorry to say that Clifford Fischer did not live to see this.

Today, my songs are as popular in the U.S.A. as they are in France. News-vendors on Broadway whistle *Hymne à l'amour* and *La Vie en Rose*, 'fans' rush up to me in the street, asking for the autograph of 'Miss Idiss', and quite a few songs have become firm favourites, including Rick French's remarkable adaptation of *Le Petit Homme*. *L'Accordéoniste*, too, is well liked and I remember one icy New Year's Day when the students of the University of Columbia had me singing it in front of the Statue of Liberty.

The Americans were slow to accept me, but I bear no grudge. There was between us, in the beginning, a mutual incomprehension . . . which brings to mind my visit to Greece.

I make no apology for lack of chronology in my reminiscences; as one incident recalls another, so I put it down.

My trip to Greece preceded the one to the U.S.A. and I should have learned from it. It should have taught me that to make a success of a foreign tour, one should first study the people and the customs of the country one intends to visit, rather than to arrive there with everything to discover.

My visit to Greece was ill-timed; I arrived in the middle of the elections. People were going to the shows, but their thoughts were centred on political matters. When I made my *début* in Athens, I soon found that the audience had very little interest in me, and although I pretended not to notice their indifference, the knowledge came as a shock. After three days, I went to see the director.

'We have each made a mistake,' I said. 'You about me, and I about the Greeks. They don't want to listen to me, so what's the point in going on with it? I think you should

84

tear up my contract while we are still on friendly terms.'

To my surprise, he did not agree with me.

'The only mistake,' he replied, 'would be for you to leave now. The worst is over. Admittedly the audiences have been disconcerted by your songs and your style ... they are so very different from our own; but they are getting used to it. If you had really displeased them, they would have let you know on your first evening here ... they would have jeered you off the stage. Keep going! In another week all will be well.'

I thought this most unlikely, but I was curious to see just what would happen and I had nothing to lose. I went on singing and eventually realized that the director had been right. My songs, which had been greeted with an indifferent, if not hostile, silence, now brought me applause, and a current of sympathy flowed between the audience and the 'pocket-sized singer' as they called me.

I have many fine memories of my Greek tour ... some rather quaint ones, too.

At one time I was singing in an open-air cinema where they were showing my film *Etoiles sans lumière,* but my songs were being spoilt by the rattling of the trams that passed every minute or two. I could hardly hear myself sing. Furiously I complained to the manager.

'I really can't see,' he said, 'what you are getting in such a state about. The trams? *They* don't even notice them. They love you. They clap until their palms bleed. What more do you want?'

Another memory of my travels; In Stockholm this time, where Les Compagnons de la Chanson and I were appearing in the second half of a music-hall presentation.

We had a wonderful audience; attentive and quick to show their appreciation. There was just one trouble; by the time I went on stage, the hall was half empty. And then I found that I was unable to hold them. Even as I sang, seats were snapping up while the audience filed quietly out of the exit.

Afterwards, when I expressed my astonishment to the manager, he said:

'It's your own fault, you know. You yourself asked to appear at the end of the programme. In Sweden, you must understand, the Star-spot is in the middle of the show, whilst later come the performers of lesser importance ... the audience usually doesn't bother to stay for that.'

I had the order of appearance changed as of the next day, and I hereby apologise to the excellent performer who was obliged to occupy the spot I had vacated. And now, of course, Les Compagnons and I were given the attention we had been denied only the night before.

On the last evening of our engagement, a member of the audience climbed on to the stage and gave me a bouquet shaped liked a heart. It was tied with a tricolour ribbon and was composed entirely of blue, white and red flowers. He hung it around my neck, while the hall cried 'Vive la France!' and the orchestra burst into La Marseillaise.

I can well imagine the cynical smiles of some of my readers. Nevertheless, when you have been singing in your mother-tongue in a foreign country and you are honoured in this way, it touches you profoundly.

Ten

*Tous mes rêves passés
Sont bien loin derrière moi,
Mais la réalité
Marche au pas devant moi . . . .*

I have now been to America so many times that there are
many theatre-wings and night-club dressing-rooms over
there which are as familiar to me as those of the Olympia
in Paris which, under the direction of my ebullient
friend Bruno Coquatrix, has re-established itself as one
of the leading music-halls of the world. But however much
pleasure I might get from recalling my appearances on
various American stages, I shall always have a very special
sort of affection for the Versailles. This, you will remember, was where I had my first success with the New-
Yorkers.

I do not like to do things half-heartedly; when I crossed
the Atlantic for the first time, I was, in effect, saying
goodbye to Europe for a while. I gave up my Paris flat
and let all the theatre managers know that it would be
some time before they would see me again. I have already
told the story of my initial failure in the U.S.A.

When it was first suggested that I appear at the
Versailles, I had hesitated. I am quite fond, it is true, of a
battle against obstacles. At the same time, I am bound to
admit that there are times when I am plunged into the
very depths of despondency, and it was at such a time that
I decided to give up my attempt to conquer America and

to return home. And then came the Versailles contract . . .
a chance to make good . . . And yet I was reluctant to
commit myself. Why? I suppose it was mostly a matter of
superstition. The very name Versailles seemed to augur
evil, for it recalled a most unpleasant memory. Unpleasant,
did I say? It brought to mind, rather, one of the most
dreadful nights of my life . . . .

We must go back in time; back to when I was only
sixteen. In spite of my youth, I was the 'manager' of a
troupe of performers . . . I assume here that one can use
the word 'troupe' to speak of three members only. This,
incidentally, was not the troupe I mentioned in an earlier
chapter, but another which I had formed with two friends,
Raymond and Rosalie.

On our posters . . . all done by hand and with somewhat
dubious spelling . . . we appeared as 'Zizi, Zozette and
Zozou; mixed act'.

One winter's afternoon, starving as usual, we arrived in
Versailles, where the Colonel of the local barracks, who
had known my father, had given us permission to put on
a show in the mess-hall after *soupe*. Having a couple of
hours to spare, we booked in at the Hôtel de l'Espérance.
We explained that we were 'artistes' and showed the
papers authorizing our evening performance; and on the
strength of this we booked rooms and got a lavish meal
on credit. This meal we did justice to as can only those
who do not know when they will get another. Afterwards,
with full stomachs and calm minds, we set out for the
barracks.

When we got to the mess-hall, we found it empty.
Patiently we waited. At last it became impossible to delude
ourselves further; no one was coming. There would be
no show.

We had not a *sou* between the three of us. We certainly couldn't get back to Paris by train. How about walking it? We thought about it but we were almost paralyzed with cold and the idea of trudging through the icy darkness was not attractive. There was only one thing to try. Perhaps the police would be good enough to put us up for the night . . . things would look brighter in the morning.

We got to the police station about ten minutes after the hotel-keeper had called to lodge his accusation of fraud against us.

We spent the night in the cells. The rest of the troupe were all right . . . they slept well . . . but not I. Only a few months earlier I had run away from my father and I knew he had reported me as missing from home. I had no identity papers[1] and I was little more than a vagabond from a legal point of view. I could just see myself being sent to a remand-home until I was twenty-one. I would have to wear the grey uniform and my head would be shaved . . . I could expect small mercy from the authorities.

We were lucky. The Chief of police was a kindly man. In the morning I told him our story. Our only crime, I explained, had been to anticipate our earnings . . . earnings which, through no fault of ours, had failed to materialize. We had acted in good faith.

He took pity on us; our thin faces, our heavily-ringed eyes, our shabby clothes and patched shoes were eloquent of themselves. He persuaded the hotel-keeper to withdraw his charge and we were allowed to leave.

That same night we put on one of our most successful shows ever. Receipts totalled three hundred francs and the following day I was able to pay the hotel-keeper the money we owed him.

It is a silly little story, I suppose, but, nevertheless, it

[1] It is illegal in France to be without *papiers d'indentité*, and vagabondage is a serious offence.

was this memory which made me loth, at first, to appear at the Versailles in Manhattan.

But nowadays, I always make the Versailles my first American stop. I go there to re-establish contact with the American public ... to prove to myself, perhaps, that it still regards me with the affection so necessary to an artiste.

Situated not far from Broadway, quite near the Waldorf-Astoria and almost in the shadow of Radio City, that gigantic and luxurious cinema of which New York is so justifiably proud, the Versailles is both night-club and restaurant. At the hundred or so tables, one can see many whose names are in the Social Register and some, even, who are, as they say over there, V.I.P.'s ... The *décor* is sumptuously rococo and the establishment increases its exclusiveness by charging highly; the *filet mignon,* for example, costs six dollars fifty cents, and a bottle of champagne sixteen dollars.

The Nile-green curtains part and there I stand, on a specially raised platform so that, in spite of my lack of inches, I can be seen by all. At first, I am gripped by an attack of stage-fright, but it leaves me as the applause dies away and an expectant silence falls in the hall.

Silence. A rather special sort of silence ... special because it is so exceptional. As the journalist Nerin E. Gun wrote the day after my first appearance at the *Versailles:*

> What is striking, is the silence which falls when Edith Piaf is announced. Americans rarely remain quiet during a show; they go on talking and ordering their drinks. Yet, for her, service is interrupted and people listen attentively. We see her, very tiny, dressed in a black taffeta frock. Her English is quaint but understandable. After each song there are cries of Again! More! and at the end young enthusiastic

girls climb on to the tables and applaud madly in the hope of getting Edith Piaf to sing just one more song.

In the same article, analysing my success, Nerin E. Gun quotes a politician who was sitting near him during my performance:

> Until now, he said, the French stars we have seen have been sophisticated images of Gay Paree, all playing on their sex-appeal. This one is different. She is a great artist with a voice that really gets you; and at the same time she's just a wan little thing who has obviously known hunger and suffering. She looks a little frightened. One can say she is the incarnation of the new European generation which is so worthy of our help.[1]

The American public is not, to judge from my own experience, so very different from the French. It is admittedly, fastidious, because on that side of the Atlantic show business has evolved to a rare degree of perfection; but this does not mean that it lacks understanding or is unappreciative of one's efforts. If you can manage a few words: or sing a song in English, the American will give you his attention. His reactions are often very spirited and he does not try to curb his enthusiasm. When he likes an artiste, he likes him or her wholeheartedly; and he is not afraid to show it.

About five minutes after you have been introduced to an American, he is calling you by your Christian name. This is, at first, surprising, but one gets used to it and soon discovers that this is his way of showing affection. He is looking on you as a friend and will do anything he can to help.

He is always in a hurry; but he is always punctual . . . this is a quality which I find commendable because I do

---

[1] A probable reference to the 'Marshal Aid' programme.

not possess it myself . . . and when he makes a promise you can be sure he will keep it. He is practical and has little time for day-dreaming, yet he is unsophisticated and easily pleased and there is a touch of just-a-boy-at-heart *naïveté* about him that I find most appealing.

He has great charm and, however surprising it might seem, this charm does not get lost in the exigencies of the great 'struggle for life' which is ever present at all levels of the American social scale. I have a personal recollection which shows this . . . .

One morning, in Hollywood, my telephone rang. A well-known film-star was ringing to invite me to go with her to a new music-hall show that evening in Los Angeles. I had made other plans and I started to explain that I would not be able to go. She didn't let me finish.

'You've *got* to come, Edith, because . . . ' and she went on to tell me that a screen personality who had once been great but who, in recent years, had fallen from the public eye, had managed to get a seven-day contract with which to attempt a come-back. If she was a success, she was to be offered another contract, for fifty-two weeks, and a full-scale U.S. tour. Everyone was expected to turn up in her support.

I, and all the others, answered the call. I saw Joan Crawford, Spencer Tracy, Elizabeth Taylor, Bette Davis, Maureen O'Hara, Humphrey Bogart, Cary Grant, Bing Crosby, Betty Hutton, Gary Cooper . . . and many others, too numerous to mention. We all gave 'Miss X' a thunderous welcome and at the end of her performance she had ten . . . fifteen . . . I don't know how many curtain calls. Needless to say, she got the contract she so badly needed.

Of course, in France too one sees similar gestures of solidarity . . . in this respect, our actors and artistes have nothing to learn from their American counterparts; but it's a pretty little story just the same.

When, after my first contact with the New York public, I was on the point of going home, part of the fault lay with a Frenchman. This man . . . I do not intend to name him . . . had lived in the U.S.A. for some years. He welcomed me avidly and took it upon himself to show me around New York. Naturally, after my first show, I turned to him for comfort . . . but I had come to the wrong person.

'*Ma pauvre Edith*,' he said, 'you should have known better. These Americans don't want to hear your tearful songs about the seamy side of life. They want cheerful optimistic numbers; with a few happy refrains you would have had them in the palm of your hand. Whatever made you undertake such a venture?'. . . and on he went in this vein until I was in a state of despair. Fortunately for me, help was not far away. It is time to mention my very good friend Marlene Dietrich.

Marlene loves France. She proved this during the dark days of the war and she has been a sort of fairy god-mother to many French artistes arriving for the first time in the U.S.A. When she saw me, worried, downcast, not far from breaking-point, she made it her duty to help and encourage me; taking care never to leave me alone with my thoughts. Because of her I was able to face up to my problems and overcome them. I have much to thank her for.

Of her great talent and her beauty, I need say little. She is the *grande dame* of the screen . . . Marlene the Irreplaceable. She is, too, one of the most intelligent women and probably the most conscientious artiste it has ever been my fortune to meet. At rehearsal she is wonderfully calm and diligent; she is never satisfied with herself and always seeks a higher level of perfection. Marlene has such personality that she could easily get by on the strength of it; but she strives endlessly to attain greater comprehension of that 'sense of theatre', that 'touch'. . . call it what you will . . . so essential to genuine success. Marlene has a charming sense of humour. I remember a time at the Versailles when she was in my dressing-room while I was changing. Each time someone knocked at the door she would open it a little and stick her head out . . . .

'What can I do for you, Monsieur? I am Madame Piaf's secretary.' And the caller would go away bewildered. The game went on until the journalist Robert Bré knocked. Marlene looked out and said her piece.

'Ah,' replied Robert, 'I didn't know. And I suppose she has engaged Maurice Chevalier as chauffeur!'

Robert Bré, of course, comes, from Belleville, a part of Paris where the boys are noted for their quick retorts. I know Maurice Chevalier would not deny this . . . he comes from the same part!

Eleven

Un refrain courait dans la rue,
Bousculant les passants.
Il s'faufilait dans la cohue
D'un p'tit air engageant . . . .

It was a great moment for me when Charlie Chaplin came
to hear me sing at a cabaret in Hollywood, because to sing
before him had been one of my ambitions for some years.
Chaplin is not a great lover of night-life . . . certainly not
a fan of cabaret . . . and when they told me that he was
sitting out there near the stage, I knew that this was to be
the special occasion I had wished for, albeit unconsciously,
for a long time.

That evening, strangely enough, I did not get my usual
attack of stage-fright. I had never met Charlie Chaplin but
I had seen his films time and time again and this was
enough to reassure me. I would be singing before a genial
man whose own work was a noble monument to the spirit
of mankind. Here, I knew, was a big-hearted man who was
sensitive to the misfortunes of lesser men. I had nothing
to fear from him. If he had come to hear me, it could not
be to disparage but only to try to understand. I could look
upon him as a friend. My voice might not overwhelm him
but there would be an affinity . . . a bond of understanding
. . . between us.

I don't mind admitting that I sang just for him that
night, and, in spite of a feeling of inadequacy, I believe
that never before, or since, have I sung so well. I put every-

thing into my singing. There was something I wanted to convey to him ... I had to make my singing say 'thank you'; thank you for the moments of intense feeling he had given me. This would be my way of saying: 'You know, Charlie, this 'little fellow' you have created is as dear to me as he is to you yourself. He has made me laugh because you planned it that way. But I have not been deceived by him. I have seen the tragic side of the story. Through him, you teach courage and hope ... and because of this I am very happy to be able to sing for you.'

After the show, Chaplin and I talked for a while ... no ... I exaggerate ... actually he did all the talking. He told me that my singing had touched him in a way that few singers had done. Coming from him, this was a precious compliment and yet I was quite unable to tell him so. I found myself completely tongue-tied. I just blushed and spluttered ... ah! I was not very brilliant that night. Later, as you can imagine, I was absolutely furious with myself.

After the poor showing I had made, I was astonished when, the next day, Chaplin telephoned me and invited me to visit him the following day at his house in Beverley Hills.

Normally I am a late riser; I like to lounge in bed, as do most people whose profession keeps them up most of the night. However, on the day I was to visit Chaplin, I changed my routine. I was up at seven, curling my hair, trying on dresses and hats ... titivating myself until I just didn't recognise myself ... although I was not expected until after lunch.

I had a wonderful time there. Charlie is a most unpretentious man and his conversation is delightful. His voice is pleasant and never forced; his gestures are restrained and there is almost a certain timidity about him. He soon put me at ease by recalling his music-hall days when he

96

Louis Gassion, Edith's father

Edith at Bernay in 1919, aged four

An early publicity photograph, dedicated to Camille Ribon in 1935

With Yves Montand, her co-star in the 1945 film *Étoile sans lumières*, directed by
Marcel Blistène

At home in 1954, striking a pose from *Bravo pour le Clown*

Edith writing song lyrics in 1954

Arriving at Orly on her way back
from New York, 7 May 1956

Edith playing table football with her husband Jacques Pills in 1954

A portrait from the 1950s

Poster for *Milord*

Poster for *Hymne à l'amour*

Olympia, 1958: Signing albums in the presence of
Mijanou Bardot, sister of Brigitte

Poster for *Mr. Saint Pierre*

Poster for *Bravo pour le Clown*

Poster from *Les Trois Cloches*

Edith with Eddie Constantine and Charles Aznavour during the television broadcast of Henri Spade's *Le Théâtre de l'XYZ*, 13 January 1951

Rehearsing on 13 January 1951

Edith taking part in a radio
broadcast during the 1950s

Edith wth Jean Cocteau during rehearsals for his play
Le Bel Indifférent in 1940

Edith in front of a portrait painted by her husband, singer Jacques Pills

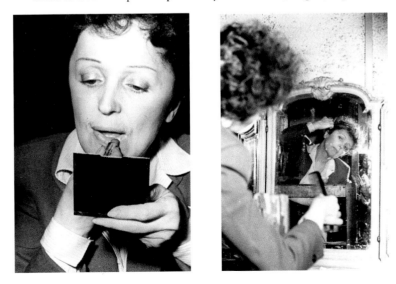

A last look in the mirror before meeting her public

Examples of record sleeves and posters for various singles

Sleeve for single accompanied by
Charles Dumont

Poster for
Non, je ne regrette rien

Various posters

Edith
Piaf

o **EMPORTE MOI**
o **LE PETIT BROUILLARD**
o **LA MUSIQUE A TOUT VA**
o **A QUOI ÇA SERT L'AMOUR**

avec

Théo
Sarapo

lumbia   Photo SAM LEVIN

Sleeve for duet with Théo Sarapo, her second husband

Polydor

LE DISQUE DE L'ÉLITE

Polydor's record sleeve for *La Môme Piaf*

Edith during a radio broadcast in 1951

Arriving at Orly airport on 7 May 1956, with Marcel Blistène,
Jacques Bourgeat, Jacques Pills, Bruno Coquatrix and Félix Martin

Orly, 7 May 1956, with Félix Martin

Olympia, 1961: A miraculous come-back

The photographs in this book are reproduced by kind permission of Les Amis d'Edith Piaf

appeared in the Fred Karno act . . . long before he had even thought of going into cinema work. Later he spoke at great length about France. He loves France . . . 'not only,' he said, 'because the French have always appreciated my films, but because to me the country epitomizes gentleness and freedom.'

Then, with no little talent, he played some of his own compositions to me on the violin. When I left him, I was so happy to have met him and even more happy because I had found him to be just as I had imagined.

'Edith,' he said, as I got into the car, 'one day I'll write a song for you . . . words and music.'

I am quite sure that he will keep his promise and that the song will be a fine one.

I did not make my mark as a brilliant conversationalist when I first met Chaplin; and I was very little better on the occasion when I had the great honour of being presented to the future queen of England . . . Princess Elizabeth.

During a visit to Paris, the Princess expressed the desire to hear me sing. One Sunday night after my performance at the A.B.C. I found myself in one of the most select cabarets on the Champs-Elysées before a very small and exclusive audience.

I was naturally nervous . . . and became even more so when, after I had sung, a young officer came with an invitation for me to join the princess at her table. As I followed him on legs which seemed to be made of jelly, I tried desperately to marshal my thoughts. How should one speak to a princess? Should I address her as 'Princess', 'Madame', or what? And was I supposed to curtsy? Could I possibly go through with it without making a fool of myself? I was terribly confused and I was certain that protocol was going to receive a bad mauling during the next few minutes.

I have no recollection of how I greeted the Princess ... but I certainly hope the *chef du protocole* was not looking. Did I go down on one knee? I don't remember. I only remember the Princess talking to me in French ... she speaks the language beautifully ... and inviting me to sit beside her. As my friends will tell you, I am quite a talkative person normally; but I could hardly think of a thing to say except by way of excusing myself for my performance.

'You know,' I said, 'I am rather tired today. On Sundays at the A.B.C. we give two *matinées* and an evening show .... did you know that?'

The princess smiled reassuringly. I blundered on: 'That means forty-two songs between three p.m. and midnight. It's quite a job. You really ought to hear me when I've not had the two *matinées!*'

I don't know how long I talked, but I am quite sure my only topic was those two *matinées*.

I made a better showing ... one does not always make a mess of things ... when I was invited to General Eisenhower's table some months before he became President of the United States. At his request I sang *Les Feuilles Mortes* ... the original French version of 'Autumn Leaves', and then we passed the rest of the evening singing old French songs. I must admit that General Eisenhower, who had spent some of the happiest years of his life in Paris, introduced me to some French folksongs that I had not previously known.

While I am talking of the great people I have met. I want to mention one for whom I feel much admiration and affection: Sacha Guitry.

During the war I was *marraine de guerre*[1] to some French prisoners in Stalag IV D. At one time, the German occupation authorities asked me and many other artistes to put on some shows in the prisoner of war camps in Germany. My first impulse had been to refuse; but after consideration I agreed. I realized that not only would I be able to bring some brightness to our boys who were dragging out their lives in the *stalags,* but I would also have the opportunity to do something practical. The baggage of an artiste rarely receives more than a superficial search and I would be able to smuggle in a few things which might help those prisoners wishing to escape. It was too good a chance to be missed.

At different times, then, I sang at the camps. I always got a great welcome and after the show the men would crowd around me while I distributed autographs, cigarettes, and certain less-innocent presents such as compasses and beautifully-forged sets of identity papers.

One day in June 1944, I had a letter from one of my 'god-sons' that the camp had been bombed with the loss of fifty French lives . . . fifty more soldiers who would not be coming home . . . fifty more families who would know more misery and suffering. I felt that it lay with me to try to do something for these families . . . put on a show, perhaps, to raise money for them. But there was a difficulty. I had been appearing in Paris for quite a long spell. People had seen me time and time again and I doubted if I could draw a large enough crowd to bring in a worthwhile sum.

I thought and thought, and then, on sudden impulse, I telephone Sacha Guitry. I had absolutely no idea what I was going to say to him, but somehow I felt that he alone could provide the solution to my problem.

[1] *Marraine de guerre*: Godmother of War; a person who had 'adopted' soldiers and who sent them letters, cigarettes and food-parcels.

I heard Sacha's voice at the other end of the line and I
began to try to explain myself.

'A couple a minutes ago, *Maitre*,' I said, 'I was full of
courage; but now I don't even know how to start.'

He was most comforting and eventually I managed to
tell him about the prisoners, the bombing, the show I
wanted to put on . . . but the hardest bit was yet to come!

'It will cost a lot to put it on,' I said, 'and by myself I
could not draw a big enough crowd to justify the expense.
What I really want to ask you is . . . would you agree to
appear? With your name on the bill we would really make
some money.'

'Where do you intend to present the show?' He asked
the question kindly and his voice was sympathetic, but as
he spoke I realized the enormity of my request. Here I was
asking the top-ranking actor to appear in cabaret!

'Well,' I replied, 'at the moment I am singing at the
Beaulieu, so I thought . . . .'

He did not let me finish; perhaps he sensed my embarrassment and wished to spare me.

'I suppose you know,' he said, 'that I have never
appeared in cabaret in my life. It would be my début and
that is a very serious matter indeed. Would you give me
twenty-four hours to think about it?'

I replaced the receiver with a sigh of relief. He had been
most kind and courteous, but I must not deceive myself;
there are certain things that one does not ask of a person
of the stature of Sacha Guitry.

And yet, when I telephoned him the following day, it
sounded almost as if he might accept.

'*Mademoiselle*,' he said. 'I have had an idea, but before
I tell you about it, I would like to see this cabaret. Is it
possible?'

'But of course, *Maitre!* Whenever you like; at whatever
time you like!'

And very shortly after, we met at the Beaulieu.

Sacha made a close examination of the stage and the auditorium and asked the electrician several questions. Then, satisfied by what he had learnt, he asked me if I had time to go with him to his home. I accepted with enthusiasm.

At length I found myself in the huge drawing-room cum study of the great master. As I allowed myself to be engulfed by an immense armchair, Sacha sat himself behind a large table on which I could see red cardboard boxes containing part of his collection of lead soldiers and carved marble hands, executed, I believe, in replica of the works of Rodin. Then he began to talk about the show which, by now, had become as important to him as it was to me.

'We will do something quite new,' he said. 'I haven't worked out all the details of my little idea yet, so we'll come back to it later. In any case, I shall recite some *Poèmes de jeunesse* and I will also think up something special for the occasion.

Blushing, I stammered:

'Then you'll appear, *Maitre?*

'Did you have any doubt?' he replied. 'How much money do you expect to make?'

I made a quick calculation.

'With your name on the bill, we can charge two thousand *francs* (about two pounds) per seat. There are two hundred places.'

Sacha pursed his lips.

'Four hundred thousand. It's not very much. But we'll think of something.'

The evening was indeed a sparkling success; the name of Guitry had attracted the *élite* of parisian society.

Towards the middle of the show, Jean Weber came on stage and announced that there would be an auction. Now an auction is not such an unusual thing, but this one, which Sacha had devised, was different. In the first place, we had nothing to sell. Sacha, anticipating that in the audience there would be many beautiful women who lacked nothing that money could buy; and that these women, having not lost their sons, husbands, and others dear to them, would be ready to express in a tangible way their sympathy for those who had lost so much. His idea had been that members of the audience should provide the articles . . . furs and jewellery . . . to be auctioned.

Five minutes after he had made the announcement, Jean Weber was digging into the pile of furs which had accumulated on the stage. He began to auction a mink coat. The articles went quickly, the bids mounting higher and higher until everyone had bought back whatever he or she had donated. At last Jean Weber announced that there remained but one item, 'the gift of a gentleman'. . . and which would not be going back to its owner. It was Sacha Guitry's own wallet containing two letters; one from his father, Lucien Guitry, and one from Octave Mirbeau; and a photograph of Sacha as a child with his father in St. Petersburg in 1890.

As the auction came to an end and I stood in the wings tearing my handkerchief into little pieces, I felt Sacha's hand on my shoulder. He was beaming.

'When Jean Weber has finished,' he said, 'you can go out there and tell them that their effort tonight has brought in no less than two million *francs*' (about two thousand pounds).

Twelve

Car tout était miraculeux,
L'églis'chantait rien que pour eux
Et mêm' le pauvre était heureux!
C'est l'amour qui f'sait sa tournée
Et de là-haut, à tout' volée,
Les cloches criaient: 'Viv' la mariée!'

I first met Jacques Pills in nineteen thirty-eight or thirty-nine. He had already made a name for himself and I had heard much about him. Then, one day, we found ourselves appearing on the same programme in Brussels. My name, as yet little known, could be seen on the posters in microscopic characters hardly bigger than that of the printer, whilst the name of Pills, and of his partner Georges Tabet, stood out in large, bold, letters. As duettists, Pills and Tabet were very popular and they had created many successes including the lovely *Couché dans le foin* by Mireille and Jean Nohain.

Together they had triumphantly toured America from coast to coast; whereas I was quite unknown outside my own country. It was only fair, then, that they should receive all the publicity and today I would be the first to admit it. At the time, however, I thought the whole thing most unjust and I used to moan about it backstage in the hope that my complaints would be carried to the ears of Pills and Tabet . . . as of course they were. I also got a little vengeful pleasure, and demonstrated my disapproval, by leaving the theatre as soon as my turn was over, and never once during the engagement did I stay for their act. My intention was to irritate them but I very much doubt if I managed to do so. Anyway, they seemed to take care never to be around while I was singing, with the result that they didn't hear me either. It was understandable. To them, I was nothing more than a name . . . and not a very big one at that.

Things were rather different when I met Jacques again, in Nice in 1941. This time I did hear him sing and my prejudices soon vanished. I realized that, in Brussels, I had greatly misjudged him. I found him, now, very appealing, and it was not long before I could see that he was attracted to me also. He never actually said so, but his eyes were eloquent enough. Neither of us was free, however.[1]

Our next meeting was in New York, some years later, where we were each appearing at a different cabaret. From time to time we met at the home of mutual friends. Although we spoke of little but the 'profession', I could read all from his very look; and I am sure that he discovered as much in mine. But the situation was much the same as it had been in Nice. The time had not yet come for us to be together.

Later, after my return to France, I heard that Jacques was divorced, and shortly after that I too found myself free. I knew then that it would not be long before Jacques and I became emotionally involved. What I could not foresee, was the way in which it would happen.

After a long tour in the United States, Jacques returned to France in the liner Ile-de-France with his American agent Eddie Lewis, who had also been looking after my interests over there since the death of Clifford Fischer.

One day, on the boat, Jacques was singing a song he had written.

'Who do you think would sing this best, Eddie?' he asked.

[1] Pills was at that time married to Lucienne Boyer.

'That's no problem! Edith, of course.'

'I'm happy to hear you say so, because I had her in mind when I wrote it; but I hardly know her and would never dare approach her with it.'

'Don't worry,' Eddie said. 'I'll fix it up when we get to Paris.'

As soon as Eddie had settled himself in the George V hotel, he telephoned me.

'It is absolutely imperative,' he said, 'that you meet someone who has composed a wonderful song for you. When can you come over?'

We arranged to meet in the afternoon of the following day, I was late, as usual, and arrived home to find in my drawing-room: Eddie, a pianist . . . and Jacques Pills.

Astounded, and a little sceptical, I said:

'You write songs?'

'Yes. Ever since high-school.'

'I had no idea. What is this latest one like?'

I was eager to hear it . . . and not only because Eddie Lewis had said it was wonderful. Although I have never been able to sing songs written by people I dislike, I simply cannot resist things written by my friends. Idiotic, perhaps; but none the less true. I only know that my instinct guards me from those who, not for lack of talent, but simply because they have no affinity with me, cannot possibly write good songs for me.

Jacques seemed embarrassed. After a slight pause he said:

'I'm not sure how you will react to the title; so I want you to hear the song first. I wrote it especially for you when I was in Punta del Esto, one of the most beautiful places in Uruguay.'

'Words and music?' I asked.

'Only the words. The music is the work of Gilbert Bécaud, a talented young man from Toulon who was my accompanist.'

The pianist played the opening notes and Jacques began to sing:

> *Je t'ai dans la peau,*
> *Y a rien à faire!*
> *Obstinément, tu es là!*
> *J'ai beau chercher à m'en défaire*
> *Tu es toujours prés de moi . . . .*
> *Je t'ai dans la peau,*
> *Y a rien à faire!*
> *Tu es partout sur mon corps*
> *J'ai froid, j'ai chaud,*
> *Je sens tes lèvres sur ma peau,*
> *Y a rien à faire,*
> *J' t'ai dans la peau!*

> (I've got you under my skin,
> I can't do anything about it!
> Stubbornly, you are there.
> However hard I try,
> You are always near me . . . .
> I've got you under my skin,
> I can't do anything about it!
> You are everywhere on my body,
> I go hot, I go cold,
> I feel your lips on my skin,
> I can't do anything about it!
> I've got you under my skin.'

I was captivated; not only by the song itself which was delightful, but also by Jacques' interpretation of it. He caught the spirit of it in such a way that, when I later added the song to my *répertoire*, I sang it exactly as he had done.

That evening Eddie Lewis and Jacques dined with me. Jacques came again the following day and each succeeding day. We worked hard at the song, striving to perfect it.

Sometimes we would refer to our previous meetings in

Nice and New York, and at such moments we would find ourselves unable to meet each other's eyes. We hid our true feelings, and when we went out together we pretended that we were only friends.

Then one day Jacques told me he loved me. And not long after he asked me to marry him. I can speak freely of my marriage because, even though it lasted only four years, I have no regrets. They were four wonderful years and I remember them with joy.

Jacques' proposal came as a shock to me and I was not able to answer him immediately. I had nothing against marriage but I believed ... as I still strongly believe today ... that marriage is incompatible with certain modes of life. It is not easy, for instance, to make a real home when your profession can drag you half-way around the world in the course of a year.

However, I became Mme René Ducos[1] on 20th September 1952. We would have liked to be married in France but the papers were not ready in time and we had a contract to go to the U.S.A. The ceremony took place in the little French church in New York and our union was blessed by an Italian-born American priest. My great friend Marlene Dietrich was my witness and I was led to the altar by my impressario and friend Louis Barrier. Our friends had organised two receptions for us: the first at the Versailles and the second at the Pavillon, the largest French restaurant in New York. But there was no honeymoon. That same evening Jacques and I each appeared on stage as usual ... he at La Vie en Rose, I at the Versailles. It was almost a symbol; just married yet already separated by our profession!

It amused Jacques to include in his programme on the day of our wedding, the song *Ca gueule, ça, madame!*[2] but

---

[1] Jacques Pills is the professional name of René Ducos.

[2] Slangy title of a song in derogation of Marriage.

I hasten to assure my readers that this was no indication of the tone of our life together. True, I have a fiery disposition and I cannot stand being contradicted. Jacques, on the other hand, is calm, placid, and conciliatory. But in spite of this great difference in our respective temperaments, I am quite certain that our marriage would have been a success had we not been so often separated by singing tours.

I was able to influence my husband to some degree and to direct his interest towards the powerful, masterly songs that suit him so well. But this does not mean that he was not already a big name when I married him. On the contrary; his very first tour in the United States had brought him the nickname 'Mr Charm'. He had carved a place for himself in the world of *chanson* just as I had, and there was never any question of rivalry between us. There was no professional jealousy when we appeared in the same programme.

For a while we believed that it would be possible for us to travel the world together; working and singing side by side. Our names were billed together at Marigny and during our tour with the Super-Circus. In America, our travels took us right across that great continent to the very shores of the Pacific. But it was too good to last. The time came when we had to admit to ourselves that our careers must separate us. Not many theatres or cabarets could afford the luxury of presenting Pills and Piaf at the same time and we would often find ourselves thousands of miles apart ... Jacques, perhaps, singing in an operetta in London, whilst my contract had taken me to New York, Las Vegas, or Paris. It was the end, for neither of us could tolerate a life of shouting *'bonjour'* to each other as our planes passed in mid-Atlantic.

But neither he nor I regret in any way those few years together, and we remain close friends.

Thirteen

> An artiste can gropingly open a
> secret door yet never know that
> behind this door lies a whole new
> world.
>
> JEAN COCTEAU

My first experience of acting was in a play by Jean Cocteau.

I had admired Jean for many years before I actually met him ... I don't think it is possible to read his work without admiring him ... and when one day some friends introduced us, I was amazed and delighted. He is a great lover of music-hall and he talked about the *chanson* with that lucidity which always surprises even those who are familiar with pyrotechnical brilliance of his conversation.

'It is at the music-hall,' Jean said to me, 'that one comes face to face with the real people ... the same people who are the fans of football and boxing. The snob in his ivory tower has had his day. Mr Everybody rules ... and he is far more interesting. He is also more fastidious.'

Before long, Jean and I were on first-name terms and an idea had begun to ferment in my mind. For Marianne Oswald, whose performance was currently the subject of intense controversy in the gallery of the Folies-Wagram, Jean had written two unforgettable *chansons parlées* ... spoken songs ... *Anna la bonne* and *La Dame de Monte-Carlo*. For Arletty, he had written a sketch, *L'Ecole des Veuves*, based on a story by Pétrone, in which she had appeared at the A.B.C. some years before the war. I now began to wonder if he would do me the great honour of writing something especially for me.

'I wouldn't expect anything of great length,' I told him when at last I dared to broach the subject. 'I can't see myself in a three-act play . . . something quite short would be admirable.'

I was thinking, although I didn't dare mention it, of *La Voix Humaine,* in which the incompatible Berthe Bovy had starred. This is what I needed . . . a *Voix Humaine* cut to my measure.

To my joy, Cocteau looked upon my idea with favour.

'Why not?' he answered. 'I'll have to think about it for a while. But I warn you; don't expect something full of wit and too poetic. I shall give you a dialogue which is straightforward and easily understood.'

The outcome of this conversation was *Le bel Indifférent.*

The play is about two people, one of whom says absolutely nothing. The scene is a shabby hotel-room lit by the glow of the neon-signs in the street. When the curtain rises, the woman is alone on the stage. She is a little nightclub singer, in love with a handsome young man who does not return her affection. She spends all her time waiting for him. She is waiting for him now. He comes home; puts on his dressing-gown; lies down on the bed; lights a cigarette; and hides himself behind a newspaper. He doesn't say a word.

Then she speaks. It is a pathetic monologue of unrequited love. She passes from anger to despondency; from sweet words to threats. She is tender . . . she rebels . . . she humbles herself. . . .

'I love you. You know I do. I love you and that is your strength. You pretend that you love me. You don't love me . . . if you did, Emile, you wouldn't make me wait

around like this; you wouldn't torment me as you do ...
going around the dives while I sit here waiting. You're
just wearing me out; there's nothing left of the person I
used to be ....'

The man has fallen asleep so she wakes him. He gets up
and dresses to go to his mistress. She threatens to kill him;
then she clings to him ....

'Forgive me! I'll behave myself. I'll stop complaining.
I'll be quiet. Let me put you to bed and tuck you in. You
will sleep. I shall watch you while you sleep. You will
dream, and in your dreams you can go wherever you want.
You can be unfaithful to me ... but please stay ... please
stay. I shall die if I have to go on waiting for you I can't
stand it, Emile; I beg of you ... stay! Look at me. I'll do
anything you want. You can lie to me ... lie as much as
you like. You can keep me waiting ... I'll wait. I'll wait
as long as you like.'

He pushes her away and slaps her face. He slams the
door as he goes out, and she runs to the window as the
curtain falls.

And that's it! A masterpiece!

Le bel Indifférent, with scenery designed by Christian
Bérard, shared the programme with another play, *Les
Monstres sacrés,* at the Bouffes-Parisiens. It came at the
end of the programme and my silent partner was Paul
Meurisse whom I had previously known in cabaret, where
he used to sing gay songs in a somewhat lugubrious manner.
With his stern face and natural impassiveness, he was
ideally cast for the play.

I started to learn my part. This was something quite new
for me, but I found the work enthralling. Then the rehearsals began. I tried not to let it show that I was very
proud of making a start as an actress ... the more so

because my part had been specially written for me by a great writer. I was not slow to realize the importance of my rôle, but I was not apprehensive about it. And anyway, Jean was there to bolster my confidence when necessary. I followed his instructions implicitly. I knew that all would go well and that I need have no fears.

At about ten o'clock on the evening of the opening-night, I was in my dressing-room, almost ready to go on stage, when a friend called to see me. I was in a gay mood and greeted him cheerily . . . much to his astonishment; he had hardly expected to find me so composed, and so confident.

'You amaze me,' he said. 'Don't you realize that you have to hold the stage by yourself for half an hour? A theatre script . . . especially one by Cocteau . . . is a bit different from a song, you know. Surely you shouldn't treat the matter so casually! There are three very great artistes out there now . . . Yvonne de Bray, Madeleine Robinson, and André Brulé. You have to follow them . . . it won't be easy. And all Paris is out in the front waiting for you.'

He said it with the best of intentions but he had chosen the worst possible moment. Suddenly, I could see the truth of his words. How could I, an amateur as far as drama was concerned, follow one such as Yvonne de Bray? I could not possibly live up to her standard. I should make a fool of myself and people would say . . . 'Serves her right. She's getting what she asked for'. And I would not be able to deny it. I was panic-stricken! I grabbed my hand-bag from the dressing-table and made a dash for the door. I couldn't go through with it; I was off; I'd hide away from them . . .

They brought me back . . . reasoned with me . . . and then, pushed by friendly hands, I found myself on stage. I was trembling and the sequence of my actions went rushing through my mind: first I had to walk up and down the room. Then I had to go to the window; put a record on the phonograph; take it off again; pick up the telephone, and say '*Allo!*' And then what? I suddenly discovered that I didn't know what came next. I had forgotten my words. My mind was completely blank! With something akin to terror I saw the time drawing nearer when I would have to speak. I would get as far as the 'Allo!' I could say it three times, perhaps four, before the audience noticed that something was wrong. Concealed in the wings, my secretary stood, script in hand, ready to prompt me should I falter . . . but how could she possibly suspect that I had dried up before I even started. The moment had arrived. I reached for the telephone . . . and as I did so, it all came flooding back. I was saved! A miracle had happened . . . there is no other word for it. And I went right through *Le Bel Indifférent* without needing the assistance of my prompter.

Did I do well that first evening? I don't really know. What I do know is that I became completely engrossed in the action of the play and in the strikingly realistic script. I didn't just act it . . . I *lived* it. And at the end as I collapsed in tears on the bed, I was absolutely exhausted.

And then the applause, and an embrace from Jean Cocteau.

The following day the press acknowledged that I had given a creditable performance in what must have been a difficult undertaking.

Unhappily, at that time . . . February, 1940 . . . theatre was going through a period of depression and *Le Bel Indifférent* ran for only three months.

I had a rather curious experience during these months of my association with the Théatre des Bouffes-Parisiens. The first part of the programme was given over to *Les Monstres Sacrés,* with Madeleine Robinson. One day,

Madeleine was rushed to hospital for an emergency operation. She had no understudy. A few hours before the show, Jean Cocteau telephoned me to ask if I would read Madeleine's part.

'I will have the script in my hand?'

'Of course.'

'All right. I'll do it!'

Nothing, I thought, could be easier. How mistaken I was!

The fear was constantly with me that I would miss a cue or make a mess of my lines . . . and I'm not saying that it didn't happen, and perhaps more than once! Anyway, I can assure you that was with genuine feeling of relief that I read the last few lines of the part, which ended with the word of Cambronne[1] And the way I was feeling, it came out very naturally . . . to the delight of the audience, which burst into laughter and applause.

I was to play again in *Le Bel Indifférent* in 1953 at the Théatre Marigny, with Jacques Pills playing the part created by Paul Meurisse. The producer was then Raymond Rouleau and Lina Nobili had designed a very beautiful set to replace the original one by Christian Bérard which had unfortunately been lost. This production was a great success and the critics spoke well of it. I shall not quote the press. But I'm sure I shall be forgiven if I reproduce here a few lines from the preface of a book in which Jean Cocteau gathered together some of his 'minor' works, including *Le Bel Indifférent* and his 'Spoken Songs'.

I have already spoken of short-rôle actresses such as

---

[1] The word of Cambronne is *'merde'*, the English equivalent of which is usually printed as 'sh . .' *'Merde'* is said to have been popularized as an exclamation of disgust or delight by General Cambronne. In France, the word is often printed in full in books, and it is always good for a titter in cinema or theatre, it is also commonly used in normal conversation.

Mlles Edith Piaf and Marianne Oswald. Without them, a play such as *Le Bel Indifférent* and spoken songs like *Anna la Bonne* and *La Dame de Monte-Carlo* would amount to very little.

Personally I disagree with this statement. *Le Bel Indifférent*, I agree, presents an actress with a wonderful opportunity to really *give,* but she can add nothing to it because nothing is lacking. The work exists in its own right. It is a masterpiece.

All the same, Jean, I am very grateful to you for writing the lines I have just quoted.

Fourteen

L' homm' que j'aimerai,
Y a si longtemps que je l'aime,
Lorsque je l'aurai,
J' vous jur' que j' le garderai.
Du moins, j'essaierai....
Les hommes sont tous les mêmes!
En tout cas, nous deux,
Nous essaierons d'être heureux.

My 'second début', as they say at the Comêdie-Francaise, was in *La P'tite Lili,* a play which required six weeks of reheasals and two years of discussion.

Mitty Goldin, helmsman of the A.B.C. for many years, had commissioned the play from Marcel Achard and was eager to present it with Raymond Rouleau as producer. Marcel Achard, however, wanted nothing to do with Rouleau, and Rouleau declared that he would never work in a theatre run by Goldin . . . especially on a play written by Achard. Achard wanted Lina de Nobili to design the scenery: Goldin had other ideas. There was a general atmosphere of dissension.

Naturally, as I was to play the leading rôle, my opinion carried some weight, and from time to time I would be consulted. I knew exactly what I wanted and I clung tenaciously to four main points: To play in this two-act musical comedy by Marcel Achard with music by Marguerite Monnot. To play it at the A.B.C. under the direction of Mitty Goldin. To have Raymond Rouleau as producer. To have Lina De Nobili design the scenery.

I got it all in the end but it took two years of patience, a lot of diplomacy, quite a few violent outbursts (to keep up my reputation and fit in with the general atmosphere), and not a little will-power ... a quality which I do not lack. At long last a settlement was reached; but now new problems arose over the casting. I saw Eddie Constantine playing the part of the gangster, but Goldin wouldn't hear of it. He considered Eddie to be gauche and clumsy. He even criticized his accent ... which was unjustified when you remember that Mitty himself, in spite of thirty years in Paris, had, until the day he died, a marked central European accent. Eventually Mitty gave way, remarking that it was always possible to make cuts in the dialogue and that anyway gangsters are traditionally men of few words and many gestures.

Pierre Destailles, the singer/composer whom Achard had considered for the part of Mario, was not available; so I suggested Robert Lamoureux, who was keen to make a start in theatre. Goldin hesitated for a long time before deciding, without enthusiasm, to give him a chance. Today, Robert is considered to be one of our best comedians.

The rehearsals, when they started, were not lacking in humour. We began work on the first few scenes, but no one knew the whole plot ... for the very good reason that the author had not yet finished it. Each day, full of zest and goodwill, Achard would bring in the next instalment, It was fascinating; just like a serial story. We used to await Marcel's arrival eagerly:

'Right, then, Marcel. Who did it? Which of us is the murderer? And little Lili; whom does she marry?'

Marcel Achard would smile and start handling out the newly-typed pages.

'Don't worry, Children,' he used to say, 'you'll find out

in good time. Now let's get on with it!' And get on with it we did.

In those days, Eddie Constantine's command of the French language was not as perfect as it is today; and during the second rehearsal Raymond Rouleau went to work on Eddie's script with his blue pencil. The part of the gangster became a silent one.

'The play will benefit,' Rouleau declared, 'and Constantine loses nothing.'

This was certainly not my opinion and I didn't hesitate to say so. I protested vehemently and there were several verbal battles in Mitty Goldin's office. I stood firm. Eddie had been engaged to act and sing; and act and sing he should. I was quite ready to give up my part, even though I might have had to pay for breaking my contract, if they would not do it my way. And I won. After a week of argument, Rouleau shrugged his shoulders and gave up the fight. Mitty Goldin, disconsolate and predicting catastrophe, left the theatre in disgust. It was some time before he would even speak to me again.

And on the opening-night, everything went beautifully. Whatever difficulty Eddie might have had with his words, his magnificent singing voice more than compensated for. The audience loved his *Petite si jolie* and made him sing it a second time:

> *Petite si jolie*
> *Avec tes yeux d'enfants,*
> *Tu boul' verses ma vie*
> *Et me donn' des tourments.*
> *Je suis un égoïste,*
> *J'ai des rêves d'enfant.*
> *Si j'ai le coeur artiste,*
> *Je n'ai aucun talent ....*
> *Voilà, jolie petite,*
> *Il ne faut pas pleurer,*

Le chagrin va si vite
Laisse-moi m'en aller!

(You pretty little thing
With your child-like eyes,
You shatter my life
And torment me.
I am a selfish man,
I have child-like dreams.
My heart is the heart of an artist . . . .
But without the gift.
Voilà, my little one,
You mustn't cry,
The pain will soon pass,
Let me go!)

Le P'tite Lili marked a turning-point in Eddie's career. Until then he had had more downs than ups, but now, although there were still a few obstacles to overcome, he began to travel rapidly to the very top. Soon after, he secured a film-contract.

We had first met some months before *La P'tite Lili* at the Baccara where I was singing. Having listened to me, he wrote an English version of *Hymne à l'amour* and brought it to me for my approval. I found the adaptation interesting . . . although some slight changes were needed . . . and the adaptor extremely likeable. On that day our '*amitié-passion*'[1] (the phrase is his) was born, and it lasted long enough to bring him luck.

He has not forgotten it. Later he published a book called *Cet homme n'est pas dangereux*. In it he wrote:

Edith Piaf taught me, as she taught others, everything about the bearing of a singer. She gave me confidence

---

[1] Amitié-passion: a mixture of friendship and ardour which leaves us in some doubt as to the true nature of the relationship.

in myself when I had none. She taught me to fight when I sought only to avoid fighting. So that I could become someone, she made me believe that I was someone.

She has a sort of genius for reinforcing the personality of another. She used to tell me repeatedly: 'Eddie, you have what it takes. You will be a great star.' And coming from her, herself a star of the first rank, these words spurred me on.

La P'tite Lili was a brilliant success from the first evening; but the press admitted this with a certain amount of reserve. Raymond Rouleau's production was excellent, they said, and there was beauty in the sets and the music. They praised the 'newcomers', Eddie Constantine and Robert Lamoureux, and the others, notably the amusing Marcelle Prince and the elegant Howard Vernon. I too received great praise. M. Paul Abram, ex-director of the Odeon, said:

> Edith Piaf might easily have continued her glorious career as a singer. Instead, she chose to launch herself into a new venture which, for most people, would have been perilous if not fatal. From her normal immobile stance, as she leans on a piano, using only her face and her arms, she has suddenly become vivacious, spritely and sensitive actress. And she has made the transition with complete success.
> Her perfect adaptation to the new medium is most striking. We all know Edith Piaf the singer, and we are familiar with the anguish of her voice as she sings of despair and love. But we have not hitherto been aware of the multiplicity of her gifts which, in *La P'tite Lili,* enable her to range from comedy of the highest order to emotion of very great depth. She is able, with no apparent effort, to portray each aspect with rare and unequalled talent.

But the praise was nowhere near as lavish when it came to the play itself. The critics weighed the play against the author's others, and found it lacking. No one seemed to realize that the author had not tried to write another *Jean de la Lune* or a new *Domino*. They could not see that although the style of the play was different, the plot was no less imaginative or ingenious.

Around the heroine, an errand-girl, a little Paris kid with a song on her lips and her heart in her hand, the author had constructed a love-story complicated by a feud between gangsters. It was a happy combination of thriller and romance written in Marcel Achard's own inimitable style. It was an agreeable blend of humour and emotion with charming scenes, plenty of wit, a lively dialogue and some delightful songs.

But although the public was well-satisfied, the critics were not. They would not accept the play as it was. They had to dig into it . . . looking for something that the author had never tried to put there. A few critics admitted that they had enjoyed the play and then went on to analyze it. Was it truly a musical comedy as the posters proclaimed? Was it not, rather, more of an operetta? Or even something else?

Marcel Achard, however, found the whole thing quite amusing. He is the sort of man who, if asked by some self-styled Dramatic Expert to define his technique, would deny that he has one. He believes that the most important thing is to give pleasure. *La P'tite Lili* was pleasing . . . it was all that mattered.

Musical comedy, operetta, or poetic fantasy, the play got away to a good start and lasted for seven months . . . the only break occurring when a motor-accident kept me off the stage for several weeks.

I do not think we've seen the last of *La P'tite Lili* and I hope to revive it one day in Paris . . . perhaps at the

A.B.C., now under the direction of Léon Ledoux. And I shall sing once more the optimistic lines of *Demain, il fera jour.*

> *Demain, il fera jour!*
> *C'est quand tout est perdu que tout commence . . . .*
> *Demain, il fera jour*
> *Après l'amour, un autre amour commence.*
> *Un petit gars viendra en sifflotant*
> *Demain,*
> *Il aura les bras chargés de printemps*
> *Demain,*
> *Les cloches sonneront dans votre ciel*
> *Demain,*
> *Tu verras briller la lune de miel*
> *Demain,*
> *Tu vas sourire encore.*
> *Aimer encor', souffrir encor', toujours.*
> *Demain, il fera jour!*
> *Demain!*

(Tomorrow will be another day
It is when all is lost that there is a new beginning.
Tomorrow is another day!
After the one love comes another.
A young lad will come whistling by Tomorrow.
He'll carry spring-time in his arms,
Tomorrow.
The bells will ring again,
Tomorrow.
You will see the honey'd moon
Tomorrow.
You will smile again,
> Love again,
> Suffer again,
> Always.
Tomorrow will be another day,
Tomorrow.)

Fifteen

At one time, when I was touring the United States and South America, I was away from Paris for eleven months.

In the beginning, it was great fun, going from New York to Hollywood, from Las Vegas to Chicago, from Rio to Buenos-Aires; but after a while I began to feel homesick and it was as much as I could do to stick to the detailed programme Louis Barrier had prepared for me.

Here and there along my route I met acquaintances and made new friends; but my long absence from France, from Paris, was slowly suffocating me. There is nothing that can take the place of the air of Paris!

Often during this period of exile I would talk nostalgically with Robert Chauvigny who had been my musical-conductor for thirteen years. We would recall this corner of the Champs-Elysées, this street of the Marais, or this aspect of the *Grands Boulevards*. It was our only means of keeping in touch, of remaining true to our city . . . and of overcoming the deadly boredom.

We had too, all the songs, the old and the new, which brought back memories of Paris. And we found a new depth of meaning in the familiar words and melodies. They became, for us, the essence of all that was the spirit of France. and, more especially, Paris.

And then, at last, the home-coming. Orly; the city outskirts; my flat on the Boulevard Lannes; my friends . . . a whole crowd of them . . . and, less numerous, my close friends!

I have always made a distinction between my friends and my confidants. I enjoy the conversation of the former; from the latter I hide nothing!

But I digress! Orly, Boulevard Lannes, my old piano, still in its usual place. I had sent word ahead of my return and soon the manuscripts of new songs would begin to pile up. Marguerite Monnot, who in my absence had written the wonderful music of *Irma la Douce*, came with her husband, the singer Paul Péri, to see me. We discussed a poem by Michel Rivgauche called *Salle d'attente*, and listened to a record of *La Foule*, a song that had already caught my attention while I was in South America. I very much wanted to sing it myself. Michel Rivgauche and Pierre Delanoe, two of my lyric-writers, also arrived, and we began work on the songs I would be singing during my forthcoming month-long provincial tour and later at the Olympia in Paris. It was at this appearance at the Olympia, incidentally, that Bruno Coquatrix asked me to stay for no less than twelve weeks . . . a record of which I am rather proud. Do you reproach me for my vanity? Remember that in the profession there is more envy than jealousy! You hear someone say 'You know so-and-so? He's been at the Olympia for so long.' or 'He was there four weeks'. I had worked hard for the Paris audience; that audience which is the world's best judge and which, whatever the future might hold, will always be 'my' public.

Speaking of 'audiences' and the 'public', I want to quote Charles Aznavour who, for some months, had been practically living at my flat, composing and writing those early works which were to bring him fame. One night as we were coming back from the Olympia, he said:

'Don't you find that the "bravos" of Paris have a savour of their very own?'

It is quite true. They are different.

Between my French provincial tour and my appearance at the Olympia, I played in a film: *Les Amants de Demain*. The scenario was by Pierre Brasseur, and when the producer, Marcel Blistène, and the director, Georges Bureau, brought it to show me, I did not hesitate. I signed up.

Later I telephoned Pierre Brasseur.

'My dear Author,' I said.

'What are you talking about?'

'Why all the surprise? You've heard of *Les Amants de Demain?*'

'You mean it is all fixed up?'

'Yes. All fixed!'

'Ah! Merde alors!'

Pierre Brasseur had had me in mind while writing his film-script and he had truly put everything he had into it. Even so, he had no idea that I would be so eager to act in it, and he was genuinely surprised that I had so readily agreed.

'Have you got a bottle of something?' he asked. 'I need a drink after that shock.'

'I hope I have!'

'Right! I'm coming to dinner. That bottle . . . I suppose it wouldn't be champagne?'

'No! I know what you like!'

At six o'clock the following morning, Pierre was still there with a glass of Beaujolais in his hand. He was quite sober and still talking. At eight o'clock, I had to ask him to go. Mme Brasseur was almost asleep and I was ready to faint with weariness. I had been beaten at my own game.

As I write these lines, the film *Amants de Demain* is waiting to be released. I don't know what the critics will think of it; but I am quite sure that it will receive a welcome from the public . . . and that is what matters. We all worked hard on the set and I have every confidence in the finished product.

The art of cinema intrigues me, and I greatly regret that I cannot devote more time to it. I could give much to it ... that I know! The *chanson* has always been the great love of my life. It ensnared me during those early days in rue Troyon and it will be a very long time before it releases me.

During my recent appearance at the Olympia, the *vedette américaine* was Félix Marten.

I met him for the first time on the return half of my provincial tour. When Louis Barrier told me about him and began to explain that he merited a place in the show, I merely replied:

'*Mon petit Loulou,* I leave the matter in your hands.'

And then one evening, at Tours, there was a knock on the door of my dressing room.

'*Bonjour, Edith.* Allow me to introduce myself. I am Félix Marten.'

He was tall, smiling, and full of self-confidence.

My first impression was that he was a rake.

'*Bonjour,*' I replied.

'I am happy to be in the show with you,' he said. 'And I would just like to say "thank you".'

'Don't mention it,' I replied, and he went back to his own room.

When the stage-manager called him, I went back-stage to listen. I can't say I was over-enthusiastic at first; but I listened the next day and the day after that. I didn't like his songs at all; but his personality was not displeasing.

One day I told Louis Barrier that he should try to arrange for Félix to appear in our forthcoming programme at the Olympia. At first Louis objected; but I pointed out that we had more than a month to transform Félix ... to change his style. I telephoned those two well-established song-writers, Marguerite Monnot and Henri Contet, and Michel Rivgauche. They came to see me and immediately set about writing some new songs for Felix. We all got down to work. Felix was not easy material, but if he was at times stubborn, he also had plenty of good-will.

The critics were divided in their opinions about the transformation we wrought in Felix Marten; but the public loved him!

Those who wonder why I sometimes take it upon myself to take a singer and remould him, have never experienced the intense joy of a sculptor who gives form to his stone, or of a painter who brings life to his virgin canvas; for had they experienced this, they would have no need to wonder. I love to create, and the more difficult the task, the greater my joy.

There is such satisfaction in learning . . . and in giving . . . .

Sixteen

I salute the *chanson*, for it is the medium through which the poet is able to communicate with the people.

Paris would cease to be Paris if the nocturnal train of her gown were not garlanded with *chanteuses* . . . those wonderful brown-, blond-, and red-headed girls who interpret the poetic soul so easily, yet so profoundly. The songs they sing appear to have no source, no author; they seem to spring quite naturally from the very macadam of the streets.

And their charm and influence is increased by the radio. The spirits of those amplified voices pursue us to the quays of Marseille and Toulon, imprinting their refrains on our hearts.

JEAN COCTEAU

I have already explained how I select my songs and why I believe the words to be of primary importance.

When, as often happens, I am asked to explain how I set about the interpretation of a song, I am perplexed, for the truth is that I rely on my instinct. I would not go so far as to say that my songs are self-creating on the stage, yet even this is partly true.

When I make a start on a new song, I work at the piano; learning words and music together. So, gradually, and without any searching on my part, the 'feeling' comes to me. Perhaps I find myself making a certain gesture at a particular point in the song; and if that gesture comes naturally the next time, I know that it is a good one. I discard any gesture which does not add something to the song. I never practice in front of a mirror. Many singers, including Maurice Chevalier, who specialize in songs of a lighter, more humorous nature, find the mirror method of great assistance, for they must calculate with great precision the impact of each gesture.

For them, mime is a part of the presentation and should be planned rather than improvised.

This, however, does not apply to the songs I sing. My movements must be genuine . . . sincere or they are valueless.

The final touch comes only when I face my audience . . . and even then it is never quite 'final'. I am always aware, of course, of the reaction of my audience; but I cannot say that it really influences me. If I feel a 'resistance', naturally I ask myself why it should be so. Marcel Achard once said that there are times when an audience lacks 'talent'. I tend to disagree; can two thousand people be wrong? I think not, and if they do not like a song, there must be a reason. It is up to the singer to search for it. It often takes time; but it can be thrilling and rewarding. The important thing is not to discard a song simply because it is not immediately successful but to persevere, and this I have always done. The public is often taken by surprise when something new is introduced, and a certain amount of coaxing is necessary. It is because many artistes . . . myself amongst them . . . have struggled to impose our new songs that the *chanson* has evolved so wonderfully over the past twenty years or so.

If, while I am singing, I become conscious of my actions, or feel that my gestures are deliberate, I know that I am losing that essential spontaneity and that the time has come to put that particular song aside for a while.

For a long time I kept a miniature piano in my dressing room, and on it I would practise musical exercises. I once astonished Marguerite Monnot by playing, by ear, the first few bars of Beethoven's Moonlight Sonata ... with a few extraneous flats, I must confess.

I never learnt music; but I adore it! I would have travelled thousands of miles to hear the great Ginette Neveu who died so tragically in the very same air-disaster that killed my very dear Marcel Cerdan.[1]

Ever since I discovered it, classical music has been for me a source of consolation, joy and hope, and I shall always be grateful to Marguerite Monnot for introducing me to Bach and Beethoven. They are my favourite composers.

Listening to Bach I become oblivious of my environment. I float on clouds of rapture and all that is sordid and base is left far behind. When I am tired of living, I have only to put on a record of Beethoven. My burdens are lightened by the wonderful music and my courage returns.

Beethoven, Bach, Chopin, Mozart, Schubert, Borodin ... I love them all, and when, all too rarely, alas, I go away for a holiday, I always include in my luggage a selection of records to listen to in the peaceful atmosphere of the countryside. And sometimes, when I am feeling pleased with some achievement, I sing, for my own pleasure, the melodies of Duparc, Fauré and Raynaldo Hahn.

I hope *my* composers will forgive me!

[1] Marcel Cerdan: World Champion boxer (he fought and beat Tony Zale by a knock-out for the World Championship in New York) whose association with Edith Piaf caused a world-wide sensation. He died in an aeroplane crash in the Azores in 1949.

Books, too, give me great pleasure. I have always loved reading. When, as a child, I travelled around with the Caroli circus, I used to spend all my spare time in the caravan reading everything I could lay my hands on. You can imagine what rubbish that was. It was not until I met Raymond Asso that I began to know the real meaning of the word 'literature'.

Raymond opened the door to a new world, a world which I was later to explore fully with Jacques Bourgeat.

I met Jacques in the days when I was singing at Leplée's. I was not yet twenty. 'Jacquot' says that at that time he was already past his prime; but this is untrue. He was about fifty. I was poor and shabbily dressed . . . his only assets were some non-existent royalties from an imaginary publisher on a book yet to be written. He became my mentor, preceptor and spiritual guide.

Jacques is the author of several authorative historical works. He has also written a charming book of poems . . . *Au Petit Trot de Pégase* . . . and uses the *Bibliothèque Nationale* whenever he pleases. He knows everything!

From him I learned about philosophy and acquired an appreciation of literature and poetry. Once we spent a holiday together at a little inn in the Chevreuse Valley, not far from the ruins of the Abbey Port-Royal-des Champs.

Later, Jacques wrote this about it:

Far from the noise, far from the world, with only a pile of books for company; near the woods where roam the spirits of Pascal, Racine and Grand Arnauld, an old man and a young girl recall and measure the spent years. It is a time of study. From the writings of Saint-Beuve they learn about those great figures of French literature who once frequented the region and who, in spirit, linger yet. Molière scratches at the door, then enters, accompanied by the immortal characters he created: Alceste, Agnès Chrysale and Sganarelle . . . Thomas Diafoirus and Argan, whom Piaf detests, are denied entrance. Jules Laforgue is there too, supported by Rimbaud, Baudelaire and Verlaine. Ronsard reads his book about love, and La Fontaine his *Deux Pigeons*. Even Plato is there, carrying his *Apology* and his *Banquet* under his arm. What a noble company! And how wonderful those evenings before the log fire as Piaf draws from these books the riches of knowledge, omitting nothing . . . forgetting nothing.

I believe in God!

Quite early in my life I learned the meaning of the word 'miracle'. When I was four years old, an attack of conjunctivitis blinded me. At the time, I was living in Normandy, at the home of my grandmother. On 15th August, 1919, she took me to Lisieux and we prayed together at the foot of the altar of little Ste Thérèse.

'Have pity on me,' I murmured. 'Give me back my sight.'

And ten days later, at four o'clock in the afternoon, I saw again. Since that day, I have always carried the image of Ste Thérèse with me.

I have another talisman, a cross with seven emeralds, which is just as precious to me. This I received from Marlene Dietrich one Christmas when I was in New York. With it, she sent a sheet of parchment with the words:

> One must find God.
> Marlene.
> Rome.
> Christmas.

Because I believe in God, I have no fear of death. There

was a time, some years ago, when I even wished for it. My whole world had been shattered by the death of one I loved (Marcel Cerdan) and I thought I could never again know happiness or laughter. I had lost all hope and courage. Faith saved me.

When the great champion to whom I was so closely bound was killed, I already knew that because others who loved him would suffer, I could never find a lasting happiness with him. His death was yet another blow. I was only saved by my faith.

Seventeen

Whom do I fear most?
Those who do not know me
and who speak evil of me

PLATO

Friends tell me that these recollections would be incomplete without a few notes on my everyday life.

Misinformed journalists have frequently made errors in the past when writing about me. One, for example, wrote that I sleep in the bed that belonged to Mme de Pompadour. This is not so. True, I had at the time a Louis XV-style bedroom . . . but it had been built much later, during the reign of Louis-Philippe.

I have a large ground-floor flat in boulevard Lannes. I am right on the edge of the Bois de Boulogne and my windows look out on to the Auteuil race-course. My front garden is quite tiny.

I occupy only three of the nine rooms in my flat; bedroom, drawing room and kitchen. I am often advised about furnishing it; but work takes up most of my time and there is little left for home-making. It doesn't bother me; I am quite content to camp out in my flat and I am not in the least disturbed by the trunks that litter my drawing-room. My essential pieces of furniture are the piano, a record-player, radio and television set, comfortable armchairs and a few low tables to hold glasses. An interior decorator would not be impressed by my home, and I must admit that the furnishings do not form a complimentary background for the few beautiful paintings which hang on the walls.

There is little I can do about it. A part of me is still very bohemian and, living as I do . . . a few months here, a few months there . . . I am unlikely ever to change.

Yet in some ways I am rather bourgeois. I am extremely sensitive to cold; from the moment the leaves become tinged with autumn, all my windows are shut tight and the central-heating turned to maximum. And I knit. Jerseys. I never stop . . . and according to my friends I never finish one. It may be true.

I hate time and its tyranny.

My day begins towards the end of the afternoon. At four o'clock I open one eye. By evening I am fairly wide-awake. I might nibble at something before my performance; but my first real meal comes around mid-night. Friends . . . usually the same ones . . . eat with me in the kitchen. We have coffee . . . I am a real addict . . . then we go into the drawing-room to make music, sing and talk. These are the hours of relaxation. There are jokes and laughter. I can take a joke. I am naturally a gay person. There was so little humour in my childhood; now I am catching up with it.

I work too, at this time. Composers bring their latest works. I rehearse new songs and scribble ideas for others on odd scraps of paper. And so it goes on until dawn breaks. By that time, only the stayers are left. The others have dropped out of the race and have either left quietly or are fast asleep in armchairs.

Am I fashion-conscious? Of course I am!

At home I am happy in my slacks and a sweater; but I love to dress up or to spend a few hours at the *couturiers*. I don't often wear a hat; but I have a passion for them and I have a large collection.

Years ago, when I first appeared at Bobino's, I wore

a simple black dress on the stage. I have worn the same one ... or, rather, replicas of it ... ever since. A more glamorous dress might distract the attention of my audience.

For certain songs, however, I have been unfaithful to the little dress that I think of as my 'uniform'. I wore a full-length black velvet gown when I sang *Le Prisonnier de la Tour:*

> *Si le roi savait ça,*
> *Isabelle!*
> *Isabelle, si le roi savait ça ...*

> (If the king knew of it,
> Isabella!
> Isabella, if the King only knew ...)

I have little more to say.

Maurice Chevalier, in his own book *Ma Route et mes Chansons,* says of me:

> Piaf, that little bantam-weight champion, drives herself unmercifully. She does not conserve her strength any more than she conserves her earnings. She races, rebelliously and unconcernedly, towards pitfall after pitfall. I foresee them; and I sympathize. But she goes on, eager to embrace every experience ... repudiating all the ancient laws of caution which are the code of an artiste.

It may be so, Maurice. But I am what I am.

President Eisenhower, when advised by his doctors to spare himself, told them that they were asking too much.

'Better to live than vegetate,' he added.

I like the the phrase. I adopted it a long time ago.

Conclusion

Better live than vegetate! This was the final note of Edith Piaf's autobiography, which she wrote in 1958. This was her philosophy of life and she practised it until the day of her death in October 1963.

Of her all-too-short life, only five years remained. In England, we at long last opened our insular hearts to her and marvelled at the power of her voice and the range and depth of her emotions.

In spite of failing health, she now recorded some of her greatest songs: 'Exodus', 'Milord', 'No Regrets', and in a world where success if often measured in revolutions-per-second, Piaf had finally 'arrived'.

Always a friendly woman; always a woman who *needed* friends; she found that as her health deteriorated, her circle of close friends narrowed and she often felt alone and unwanted. She became convinced that Providence, for so long on her side, had now grown tired of her and that the end was not far off.

All her life she had loved and had searched for love ... for true happiness. Often, she thought she had found it; but disillusionment was always just around the corner. Men came and went; each one adding a little more happiness, a little more understanding, a little more despair.

But there was to be one last chance. In October, 1962, in the face of wagging tongues and sagely nodding heads, she married Théo Sarapo, a young singer some twenty years her junior. Once more there was love in her life; a love which, she said, was the true, complete love she had for so long sought. With her Téo, Piaf spent the last twelve months of her life. They sang together; made records together; and together they appeared at the Olympia in Paris.

And then ... *s'était fini!* Cocteau's 'Nightingale' was dead ... and the world was that much poorer.

AFTERWORD BY MARGARET CROSLAND

. . . But the world has not forgotten Edith Piaf. In the winter of 2003, forty years after her death, her life and achievements were commemorated in a comprehensive, moving exhibition at the Hôtel de Ville in Paris. It was well attended, because her fame had not suffered after her early death, in fact it had grown, thanks in part to the recording industry, which brought her a world-wide audience, including old admirers – who had seen her on stage in Europe and in North and South America – and to the many young people, who now heard her voice for the first time in both songs and taped interviews. They were immediately enchanted.

Musicologists, including the late Marc Robine, who presented the new French edition of this autobiography on the occasion of the fortieth anniversary of Edith's death, carried out valuable research on various aspects of the singer's life and work, establishing the truth about some of Edith's favourite legends. As her songs – and in fact the whole of her life – prove so clearly, she loved drama: she could never accept the so-called truth if it was less impressive than the fiction. Most of her admirers, like Edith herself, have preferred to believe that she was born on the street – and the plaque on the wall of number 72, rue de Belleville appears to confirm that fact – but, as I discovered in 1985, her birth actually took place at the nearby Hôpital Tenon. Another fable about Edith's personal life, her 'blindness' when a schoolgirl, cured, she believed, by the intervention of St Theresa of Lisieux, was no more than conjunctivitis – but at least the comforting words of the saint influenced Edith

139

throughout her many illnesses and emotional problems. The singer's religious faith was intense, though she was never received into the Roman Catholic Church.

One more myth, not directly attributable to Edith herself, has also been clarified: the claim by Simone Berteaut that she was Edith's half-sister. She was indeed the companion of those struggling, poverty-stricken years when she and Edith earned a pittance by singing in the streets and army barracks, but, as Edith's family have constantly insisted, they were, in truth, in no way related to one another.

Marc Robine also enhanced the original text of the book, which she wrote with the help of René-Louis Dauven, a Radio-Cité journalist who also wrote for *La Vie parisienne* – by adding minor corrections to passages where Edith's memory had deserted her and where he had access to information of which she probably had no knowledge. The revised French edition concludes with moving reminiscences by Fred Mella, the last surviving member of the Compagnons de la Chanson, reminding readers of how Edith took this group of young men in hand, persuaded them to change their repertoire and so brought them fame.

Inevitably the early biography did not include personal details about Edith's lovers, most of whom were still alive in 1958 when the book was written. However – and this is probably the most interesting aspect of the book – she describes in detail her professional relationship with some of them, notably her encounter with Yves Montand, who owes his breakthrough and early success almost entirely to her. Readers will not find here any mention of the men she met in Greece, in the United States or the many she knew and loved briefly in France, but her description of her four-year marriage to the singer Jacques Pills is both fair understanding and, like every instance in Edith's life, inseparable from her professional existence.

The last year of her life, with its happy marriage to Théophanis Lamboukas (lovingly dubbed Théo Sarapo by Edith), a man much younger than herself, was again dominated by professionalism, for she trained the ex-coiffeur to appear with her on stage and sing new songs that will always be associated with this partnership. Another aspect of her dedication to her professional life was her continued search for new composers and librettists, including Charles Dumont, and Francis Laï.

Although Edith understood that her admirers were always delighted to hear her sing the classic songs that had made her reputation in the early days, she wanted to go further, make new discoveries and find new songs to which she could do justice even as she and her voice grew, inevitably, older. Her repertoire was extensive, amazingly so – some two hundred songs that she sang and recorded, including thirty for which she wrote the all-important lyrics. However, she understood that fashions and tastes moved on and realized that she would have to change and develop, too, until the end of her performing life. This was another aspect of her all-consuming professionalism, which has been responsible for keeping her memory alive far more than has gossip about her emotional relationships – although such relationships are an essential element in the world of *la chanson*.

When unhappy love affairs and the death of Marcel Cerdan overwhelmed her, the emotion she felt and generated in others passed directly into the dynamism and sheer magic of her performance on stage. And the death in a car crash of the widowed Théo, seven years after her own, seems almost yet another disaster in her emotional life, as though her existence had been mysteriously prolonged to include the last man she loved.

Edith Piaf's continued fame and the affection of her fans are surely the result of her intense dedication to work and to the range of her interpretations – truly dramatic but always carefully controlled – that have never been surpassed. Others may sing her songs, but she was unique; she cannot and will not go out of fashion. That is why these recollections, which keep her own thoughts and her speaking voice alive, are so instantly readable, lasting and invaluable.

Also published by Peter Owen

Nearer the Moon

Anaïs Nin

0 7206 1206 3 • cased • illustrated • 400pp • £25

'Fully conveys a life lived at white-hot
intensity . . . a psychological and
literary triumph.' – *Chicago Tribune*

**A feminist icon who pushed the
boundaries of women's writing in
terms of both form and content,
Anaïs Nin has long been
celebrated for her diaries which
revealed her private self, her
doubts and weaknesses and the
uncensored details of her
relationships.**

This fourth volume of *A Journal of Love* follows *Henry and
June*, *Incest* and *Fire* to cover the years 1937–9 when she was
aged thirty-four to thirty-six. It continues the story of what Nin
called her 'dismemberment by love'.

She remains torn between three men: the writer Henry Miller,
whose detached self-immersion and artistic amorality both
attract and repel her; a passionate Peruvian, Gonzalo Moré,
who is a sensitive and attentive but jealous lover and who
drives her to distraction; and Hugh Guiler, her faithful
husband.

The diary ends with Nin's departure from France as war
looms. She has no idea that she will never live in France again
and that this is the last diary to be written there.

Also published by Peter Owen

The Miscreant

Jean Cocteau

0 7206 1173 3 • paperback • illustrated • 163pp • £9.95

'Butterfly-like, brilliant, febrile . . . Cocteau's famous novel was all but a bible to avant-garde intellectuals of the 1920s.' – Elizabeth Bowen, *Tatler*

'It is the book's universality that engages us: its persuasive account of Jacques' first love affair with the revue artiste Germaine and his discovery that sexual behaviour is far too complex not to contradict the dreams of an adolescent.'
– *Times Literary Supplement*

Jacques Forrestier, the central character of Cocteau's famous first novel of 1921, is a bisexual parasite and dilettante.

Leaving his provincial family, he comes to Paris to study for his degree. Indulging in a life of dissipation with a group of students and their mistresses, he falls in love with Germaine, a chorus girl kept by a rich banker. The affair, doomed from the start, forces Jacques to come to terms not so much with society as he finds it but with himself.

A sparkling evocation of the Parisian scene of the 1920s, *The Miscreant* is also a study of loneliness and youthful disenchantment. It is a perfect showcase for the savage irony and epigrammatic wit that consistently distinguish Cocteau's brilliant and highly individualistic prose style.

Translated from the French by Dorothy Williams
With illustrations by the author

Erotica

Jean Cocteau

0 7206 1181 4 • paperback • illustrated • 110pp • £13.95

'These erotic drawings are replete
with Cocteau favourites –
well-endowed teenage sailors
disporting themselves in a blatantly
sexual manner . . . delectable.'
– *Gay Times*

'Lavish . . . a fitting tribute to sexual
love and a defiant expression of
sexual liberty.' – *Him*

**The majority of drawings in this volume – obsessional,
worshipful and sexually explicit – could not be published in
Jean Cocteau's lifetime. Before the first publication of *Erotica*
in the early 1990s, few of these images had been seen before
in Britain.**

Cocteau's models were from a variety of backgrounds. Some
were casual pick-ups, others were lovers and friends. Among
those represented here are his most famous lovers – the
precocious writer Raymond Radiguet and the actor Jean
Marais, as well as many of his distinguished contemporaries:
Picasso, Stravinsky, Nijinsky, Apollinaire, Sarah Bernhardt,
Isadora Duncan and Mistinguett, 'Queen of the Paris Music Hall'.

Highly revealing of Cocteau's search for his own personal
'truth', these sensitively drawn and haunting works have taken
their place beside the erotica of such artists as Picasso,
Modigliani, Schiele and Neizvestny.